Do You Know a Good Expert?

Lawyers Tell Psychiatrists What They Want

Edited by Danny Allen

Cartoon and cover design by Robbie Mills

Second edition
Copyright © 2014 Danny Allen

ISBN-13: 978-1497449336
ISBN-10: 1497449332

Disclaimer and Terms of Use: The Author and Publisher has strived to be as accurate and complete as possible in the creation of this book, notwithstanding the fact that she does not warrant or represent at any time that the contents within are accurate due to the rapidly changing nature of the Internet. While all attempts have been made to verify information provided in this publication, the Author and Publisher assumes no responsibility for errors, omissions, or contrary interpretation of the subject matter herein. Any perceived slights of specific persons, peoples, or organisations are unintentional. In practical advice books, like anything else in life, there are no guarantees of income made. Readers are cautioned to rely on their own judgment about their individual circumstances to act accordingly. This book is not intended for use as a source of legal, business, accounting or financial advice. All readers are advised to seek services of competent professionals in the legal, business, accounting, and finance fields.

Dedication

This book is dedicated to the memory of

Linda Crane

Secretary, guardian and source of wisdom

Other books by Danny Allen

We Need It By Next Thursday – The Joys of Writing Psychiatric Reports 2014

It's a Shrinking Business – How to Run a Psychiatric Practice 2014

Business for Medics – How to Set Up and Run a Medical Practice 2014

A Medical Life – A Sort of Autobiography 2016

Contents

Foreword – **Danny Allen**

I have spent many happy hours writing medical reports and just a few less training for this role. It was this work which inspired me to write my first book 'We Need It By Next Thursday – The Joys of Writing Psychiatric Reports' which I hoped would convey some of the excitement I felt to junior colleagues and perhaps encourage some of them to take up the baton. For, although we are currently going through a period of intense government negativity about experts, no-one should be in any doubt that the tide will turn again before too long. It is by way of being in the nature of expertise that people simultaneously dislike one's perceived monopoly on knowledge – yet crave it when things go 'pear-shaped'.

After I left the NHS I determined to do some of the things I did not have time for then; this book is one of them! There are numerous courses one can go on to find out about all aspects of report writing and how to behave when in court, yet I felt the market lacked a short focused book aimed at the psychiatrist to give them an understanding of what was required from our legal colleagues, particularly for people who just wanted an understanding before committing. How better to find out, then, than to ask the people who read our reports to tell us what they want from us.

Introduction – **John Wilkins**

There has been a great upheaval in the relationship between experts and courts, particularly in the Family Court arena. Never before has the spotlight been shone on so strongly on those, particularly medical practitioners and psychologists, providing expert evidence in the court system. The loss of expert immunity, the pressure on fees, the increased number of complaints made to the GMC and other professional bodies has led many to conclude that the work was more trouble than it was worth. This has led to difficulty in instructing experts particularly as experts become more conservative about the scope of their work. This will inevitably lead to poor justice for many and no justice at all for some.

Following Danny Allen's previous book, told very much from the perspective of the expert, this volume comes as a timely reminder for those who are thus involved in expert evidence work of the issues involved, the frameworks used and perhaps, most helpfully the pitfalls that await the unsuspecting expert. Moreover, I am not aware of any other book that provides guidance and advice from the perspective of lawyers. It has always been my view that lawyers and doctors speak a different language, have a different way of approaching problems and therefore anyone who is intending to provide expert evidence has to understand the world in which lawyers work and the way in which our courts approach problems. This book is therefore timely and potentially helpful to anyone intending to embark on a career as an expert witness or even for those of us who have worked in the courts for many years.

Although the landscape in the criminal justice system has not changed anyway as near as much as it has in the civil courts and in particularly the Family Court, Maxine Cole's chapter provides a very useful description of the process taking a defendant from the point of arrest to court. This chapter will provide a useful guide for those unfamiliar with the criminal justice system. It also, usefully, refers to the Police and Criminal Evidence Act (PACE), something that is often the focus of expert testimony.

Jon Nicholson's chapter on civil courts focuses, understandably, on personal injury. This is probably the area where most psychiatrists and psychologists will get involved in producing expert testimony and the chapter is a helpful digest of the fundamental principles affecting the civil courts and also provides useful reference materials. The basis of the Bolam Test, duty of care, causation and damages is particularly helpful as is the section on the joint experts report and I found it particularly useful to read the account of the rules and etiquette of talking to the different sides of the case, something that has exercised me from time to time.

The area where there has been most change over the past few years has been in the Family Court and Nadia Salam's chapter provides a useful explanation of the types of proceedings and the main players involved in any Family Court case. There is a useful explanation of the issues governing decisions made by the Family Court and what issues the court addresses when it is deciding about instructing experts. There is also a useful explanation of the scope of Family Court reports.

The thorny issue of medical records is addressed by Ali Malsher. Those of us who do expert reports are often frustrated by the lack of documentary information, the timing of the provision of medical records not to mention one's ability to read doctor's writing or decipher bad photocopying. There is useful guidance about what is expected of the expert in relation to medical records and what might or might not be relevant. I was reminded of the comment of a colleague of mine once, "Always read the papers!".

To anyone starting out on a career as an expert will want to know what to avoid in producing a report. Whilst Cyrene Aboy's chapter on this focuses on personal injury, it provides a useful basis for providing reports in any of the court forums. There is particularly helpful advice on the avoidance on the use of jargon, something that is second nature to most doctors and psychologists.

The book so far, having gone through the basics, then addresses some of the more subtle issues. Vikki Martin's chapter on the balance between evidence and opinion is particularly helpful. Again there is a very useful focus on what solicitors and courts expect from experts and perhaps most particularly what they do not want. Very useful tips on how to express an opinion and a further exposition of the Bolam test. The provision of a literature review is likely to become more common and will recall experts to pay attention to the scientific or evidential basis of their opinions. As an expert it is all very well to rely upon on one's own experience and expertise, but if it is possible to refer to peer review journals then all the better.

In addition to the changes in the Family Courts, the advent of the Mental Capacity Act has led to increasing requests for reports about an individual's capacity and Karen Shakespeare's chapter is again a useful introduction to what is expected in reports relating to mental capacity bearing in mind that this is a changing area of law. I found the template particularly useful but there are also useful tips for General Practitioners who will often get drawn into issues of capacity in relation to their patients as they are the ones that know them best.

Particular issues relating to the provision of neuropsychiatry reports are well covered in Megan Goodyer's chapter; this is particularly so in relation to issues of expertise. This is an area where it is easy for an expert to overplay their hand and portray themselves as experts when in fact they are not. There are further useful tips, perhaps the most helpful relating to the provision of draft reports. I have slipped up once or twice on this matter, to my embarrassment and discomfiture, when in the witness box.

One of the most contentious areas is in the provision of Family Court reports and particularly those relating to parents who are often being accused of abuse or neglect. Kirsty Richards' chapter provides a useful overview of how to deal with parents who are often hostile to the process and also provides useful tips in not overplaying your expertise and straying into questions of parenting ability which are most often the province of parenting assessments conducted by child health professionals and not experts.

Another area which has shown an increase in reports is in immigration cases. Leonie Hirst's chapter provides a very helpful description of the basics with a focus on the Human Rights Act, the Refugee Convention and also Immigration Detention. She provides helpful descriptions of tribunal procedures, the limits of expert testimony and also pitfalls to avoid. The potential basis for reports is also helpful for those who are perhaps doing these reports for the first time.

In Andrew Berk's chapter on employment reports, there is a good explanation of the effects of the Equality Act (previously the Disability Discrimination Act). This was the one chapter that also mentioned something that I considered to be important which is the frequently conflicting duty of an expert and the clinician who treats the patient. Although Andrew Berk does not exactly say as much, the implication is clearly that if you have a treating responsibility to a patient, providing an independent expert report is possible as the duties of an expert are primarily to the Court and the duty of care a clinician owes the patient according to the GMC guidelines are, in my opinion, incompatible.

One of the most daunting aspects of providing a report is having to meet the expert provided by the other side when there may be areas of disagreement. The chapter by Laura Millman and Katherine Pearce on experts' meetings gives useful guidance from the lawyer's perspective of what is expected from experts when they are trying to come to some sort of consensus document ,whilst also ensuring that they do not simply agree to avoid an appearance in court. If you are going to be an expert in court you have to have the courage of your convictions and be prepared to stand up in court and defend them. If you are not, then this is probably not the work for you. I can recall a colleague of mine who would never do reports for the civil courts and confined himself only to reports for the criminal courts purely on the basis that he did not consider himself temperamentally disposed to the often disputatious and hostile environment of a civil court hearing.

The simple adage of, "Stand up, speak up and shut up" is perhaps inadequate now as guidance for giving evidence in court. Shamsun Nahar's chapter on this is helpful and it reminds us of our duty to the court and not to the person that we have assessed or indeed the person who pays our bill. There is a useful guide in this chapter about dos and don'ts, which even thought I have given evidence many times over the years, I found useful and will probably keep as a reminder.

One of the major changes in the recent past has been the loss of expert immunity, something that seems to go back a very long time indeed. In fact, this chapter by Leslie Keegan provides a very interesting historical background to the question of expert immunity. None of us want to be sued ourselves and her advice about how to protect against being sued is again a chapter which is helpful to whether you are embarking on a career as an expert or have been doing it for many years. It also emphasises the issue of referring to a range of opinion. Your opinion may be entirely legitimate, but if there is an alternative opinion, which there often is in mental health, we are obliged to refer to it and to comment.

The trainee's viewpoint expressed by Sam Vhondo is helpful in the view of anyone coming to this work afresh. We are all aware of the situation where trainees see things with greater clarity and often ask questions which superficially seem naive, but which in fact are apposite. The section on the qualities that lawyers look for in experts is particularly helpful and again there is reference to confidentiality and conflicts of interest, something that tends to be overlooked at times.

The majority of experts providing evidence in court have not had accredited training for such work. Training schemes in general psychiatry, old age psychiatry and child and adolescent psychiatry do not have specific modules relating to providing expert evidence or indeed any aspect of medical jurisprudence. Most consultants have gone through a general training and their expertise is dependent upon their clinical experience and knowledge. The decision to provide expert evidence to the courts is usually a matter of personal choice or chance. It may be that a psychiatrist or psychologist is asked to provide one report in relation to a case and that report is well regarded enough for the firm of solicitors to ask that person to provide further reports in further cases and the clinician concerned gradually becomes 'an expert'. The name is quickly passed around between lawyers who ask each other, "Do you know a good expert?".

Feedback from solicitors is rare and but in these days of revalidation for doctors we have to take steps to obtain feedback from them for appraisal purposes. Nonetheless, the most potent form of feedback is whether or not you are instructed again. It has been a reasonable assumption over the years that if you have a thriving medico-legal practice, you must be doing something right. However, that is probably not enough. Individuals who are want to give expert evidence now go on courses which, whilst helpful, provide a template that is particular to the trainer concerned and may not be relevant in all settings. For instance, a medical report that is suitable in style for the criminal courts, may not be suitable for the civil courts in a personal injury case. Experts have to be much more adaptable than they tend to be in the way that they write reports.

It is clear, therefore, that anyone embarking on a career as an expert or where they have fallen into giving expert evidence almost by accident need to look around for ways in which they can accrue the relevant expertise and knowledge in order to do a good job. If accredited training for such input does not exist or only exists for those who have had training in forensic psychiatry, and the courses that are provided by the legal firms tend to be idiosyncratic, books such as this can provide a very useful guide to what is required by the different branches of the legal system. I would recommend this book to all those who intend to start giving expert evidence, either by design or chance, and to those who are already providing expert evidence but want to do a better job particularly in the current climate of increased scrutiny of expert evidence in the justice system.

Chapter 1 - The criminal legal process - **Maxine Cole**

The objective of this chapter is to provide the reader with a basic outline of criminal procedure in England and Wales. Scotland is excluded because it operates under a separate legal system to that practised in England and Wales. We will be using the fictional case of R -v- John Smith, and 'travelling' with him through the criminal justice system where he encounters criminal procedure in action. Along the way we will examine other relevant cases. But first, what is criminal procedure? Simply put, it is the set of rules and practices that govern the way in which a person, called the defendant, travels through the criminal justice system.

A night to forget

John Smith is an ordinary 25 year old man, in an ordinary job, leading an ordinary life. On one of the nights in his ordinary life John went with his two friends, Peter and Mark, to a nightclub. Whilst inside, John became involved in an argument with a male, named Charles. The argument escalated into a fight between John and Charles, with his friends and others in the nightclub looking on. The police were called, but by the time they had arrived the fight had been stopped. John was being held by the nightclub door staff, whilst Charles was being tended to by members of the ambulance service. The police conducted enquiries and asked those present what had happened. They spoke with John and Charles, who gave their accounts. John stated that he acted in self-defence whilst Charles alleged that he had been assaulted by John in an unprovoked attack. John was arrested on suspicion of causing Grievous Bodily Harm (GBH) and taken to the local police station whilst Charles was taken to a nearby hospital. John's arrest as a consequence of the allegation made by Charles signalled his entrance into the criminal justice system; but first of all what is an allegation and what is an arrest?

The allegation against John and his subsequent arrest

An allegation is a statement made to police that an offence has occurred. On being told that a possible offence has been committed, officers are duty bound to investigate the allegation made to find out whether there is any substance to it. During the course of an investigation officers will interview the suspect and complainant, as well as speak with and take statements from witnesses.

They will also gather CCTV and forensic evidence, take fingerprints and photographs of the scene amongst other things. Now, whilst some allegations are deemed to be true such as the conviction, after trial of Costadinos Constavalos, also known as Dappy from the pop group Ndubs (see R v Constavalos & others, 2012). Others, such as that made by Kirsty Debanks are clearly false. In Miss Debanks' case she told officers that she had been raped by her ex-partner Mr Newitt. Mr Newitt was held in custody for 6 hours but, fortunately for him, his alibi was corroborated by CCTV. This showed that Mr Newitt was elsewhere at the time of the alleged rape. So, on 17 May 2013 at Oxford Crown Court, Miss Debanks, having earlier admitted to lying about the rape, was sentenced to 8 months imprisonment.

So, turning back to what Charles said to the police. He told them that John had assaulted him. This, being an allegation which clearly had some merit, given that Charles was bleeding heavily from his injuries, the officers decided to arrest John because the allegation was one of an arrestable offence; plus they have to obtain John's version of events in a formal recorded interview. Now the question arises as to what is meant by an arrest?

Although an arrest is the uttering of the words "I am arresting you….." and placing a person in handcuffs if necessary, officers have to be very careful when arresting a person. This is because they have "no more right to lay hands on someone than any other member of the community" (Parker LCJ in Ludlow & other v Burgess 75 Cr). So if they grab the person and then utter the words they can find *themselves* being lawfully assaulted as happened in Collins v Wilcox. In this case, an officer placed his hands on a prostitute to arrest her, however she punched him. She was later convicted of assaulting the officer in the execution of his duty, however appealed her conviction. On appeal it was held that she did not assault the officer in the execution of his duty because the officer, when he was assaulted, was acting outside the scope of his powers and thus did not have a right to touch her before uttering the words or informing her she was going to be arrested. The fact that, in response to his grabbing her, she punched him was deemed reasonable in the circumstances. There is, as you can see from this case a very thin line between a lawful arrest and an assault being committed by an officer.

So, turning back to our fictional case involving John, an allegation of assault has been made against him, as a consequence of which he has been arrested, and he feels the first touch of criminal procedure as he enters the criminal justice system. John is then placed inside a police van and driven to the police station.

At the police station

Once at the police station John is taken into the custody area. There he meets the Custody Sergeant who takes John's personal details and opens a custody record. This is a document on which his details are entered along with details of his personal effects, notes about medical conditions, demeanour, whether he is an illicit drug user or alcohol abuser etc. It also details the care that John receives whilst in custody and whether he has undergone any testing. For example, if John had been arrested on suspicion of driving with excess alcohol, then his intoximeter reading (the amount of alcohol in his breath) would be entered into the custody record. John is then placed in a cell to await the arrival of a solicitor or police station representative to represent him in the interview, but that is only if he wants representation.

John's representative is provided with initial 'disclosure' by the officer in the case. At this stage, the officers may only have preliminary details or evidence such as the initial complaint being handwritten and contained in the officer's notebook but they have to provide details of the offence being alleged. The interview is the time when John is asked for his account of events and can either provide a full account or choose to remain silent, only stating "no comment" and submitting a prepared statement in which he denies the offence alleged and asserts a defence or John could also decide to provide a mixture of the two. However, if he chooses not to answer any questions during his interview but provides an account at trial, the judge/bench hearing the case may, draw such inferences as appear proper from his earlier no comment interview (see s34(2) Criminal Justice and Public Order Act 1994).

At the end of the interview officers may decide to bail John pending the outcome of their further investigations, which could be to collect CCTV evidence or await results of forensics. Alternatively, they could decide that there is sufficient evidence with which to charge John with an offence. If the decision is that there is sufficient evidence to charge John then the police compile a file and present it to an Evidential Review Officer (ERO) for a decision. The ERO decides whether further investigative actions should be undertaken or whether the file should be passed to the Crown Prosecution Service (CPS) for a lawyer to authorise the police to charge John. The scope of the offences that police can charge people with are outside the scope of this chapter, but are contained within paragraph 15 of DPP Guidance (5th Edition, May 2013).

In John's case, the ERO decides that there is sufficient evidence to show that Charles' injuries and the circumstances amount to s18 Offences Against the Persons Act 1868 Grievous Bodily Harm (GBH) and, as such, the file is passed to the CPS for a final decision. Meanwhile John is released from custody on conditional bail pending a final decision by the CPS.

Bail

Bail is the procedural means by which people have their liberty removed, restricted or restored. When Bail is refused at the police station the person has to remain in custody under the Bail Act 1976 until they appear before a court. This is normally within 24 hours, hence the reason why specially selected courts are open on public holidays, to process what are known as 'custody cases'. Once in court the bail position is considered afresh. This can result in a person being freed entirely, only to return to court for their trial, sentence or administrative matters involving their case, or having their liberty removed and having to remain in custody, but at a prison. In John's case he has been granted conditional bail. This means that he is free to leave the police station but has to abide by the following conditions:

i.   A curfew between 8pm and 7am – this means he must be at home from 8pm until 7am - if he is not then he risks being arrested and kept in custody until his first appearance before the court;

ii. Not to contact, directly or indirectly, the complainant, Charles

Plus, John must return to the police station on a fixed date and time where he will either be charged with an offence or informed that there is no further action to be taken against him at this stage. It should be noted that what has happened to John is not uncommon. We may consider, for example, the case of R v Philpott, Philpott & Mosley [2013]. This is a recent case where the parents and neighbour committed arson, killing six of the Philpott's children. All the defendants were placed on bail pending the CPS authorising the charges against them. But when they returned to the police station on their fixed date, they were charged and kept in police custody pending their first appearance before magistrates. They, however, did not apply for bail and were kept in custody throughout and so when they were sentenced on the 3 April 2013, they were somewhat used to their surroundings.

Charging

Once the police have sent their file to the CPS it will be reviewed by a Senior Crown Prosecutor who decides the level of the charges and produces a document of their advice and authorisation to charge called an MG3. The MG3 details the lawyer's reasons for authorising the charge by reference to the Code for Crown Prosecutors and the two tests:

i. Is there sufficient evidence to provide a realistic prospect of conviction?

ii. Is it in the public interest to prosecute?

Prosecutors must apply these tests and also consider any relevant case law, policy or guidelines before concluding that a person should or should not be charged. John's file is passed to the Crown Prosecution Service who, contrary to the ERO decision that it was a s18 GBH, has authorised that John is charged with s20 GBH contrary to the Offences Against the Person Act 1868; this is a lesser offence. They have also drafted the charge for the officer to put to John for when he attends the police station on his return date. When John is charged he was bailed for a second time, but this time he has added restrictions placed upon his liberty. On his bail sheet this time are two further conditions:

i.   Residence at his parents address
ii.   Not to go within 100 metres of the Ordinary Public House, in So So Lane.

John's first appearance in court

The first court John appears in is the Magistrates' Court. Here he is placed in the dock and asked by the clerk to confirm his name and address. The clerk is a lawyer who sits below the bench where the magistrate sits. The clerk advises the lay magistrates and assists judges on points of law or other matters that may arise during the course of the court's business. It is quite a powerful position, the power of which Mr Munir Patel exploited to the full. Mr Patel was a clerk who dealt with traffic offences. In 2011 Mr Patel was sentenced to 3 years imprisonment for bribery and misconduct in a public office. What he had done was to accept payment for advice on how to avoid being summoned for traffic offences and prevented traffic penalties being entered onto the legal database.

The clerk then reads the charges to John and asks him if he wishes plead guilty, not guilty or to make no indication to the GBH offence. This is because GBH is an 'either way offence' which, means that it can be heard in either the Magistrates' Court or the Crown Court.

Although there are three options, what happens next falls into two streams. If John pleads guilty, the court is told the facts of the offence and the details of any previous convictions. They would then listen to any mitigation submitted on John's behalf by his representative. Having heard the facts and mitigation the court will proceed to sentence. The case may be adjourned for a pre-sentence report (by Probation) so that his personal circumstances and any sentence options can be examined including the possibility of his committal to the crown court for sentencing.

If John pleads not guilty or makes no indication, the court proceeds to *mode of trial*. Here the prosecutor presents the

Crown's version of events and any other relevant factors. The defence also make representations but the Crown's case, at its highest, is taken.

The judge/lay magistrates then use what they have been told and the Magistrates' Court Sentencing Guidelines to decide which court should hear the trial (also known as deciding jurisdiction). If it is decided that the case should be heard in the Crown Court then the case is adjourned for committal. However, this procedure changed in 2013 and now the majority of cases should remain in the Magistrates' Court with only the most serious, or those at serious risk of receiving a custodial sentence, being sent to the Crown Court to be dealt with.

The issue of bail is also dealt with and, if the defendant is in custody, the clerk and prosecutor confirm the number of days left before which a trial must be held. Once committed John's next appearance will be at the Crown Court.

At the Crown Court

The indictment is read and the defendant is asked whether he pleads guilty or not guilty. If he pleads guilty he is sentenced either immediately or the case is adjourned for a pre-sentence report into whether the defendant has any issues. If these include drugs, alcohol or mental health problems, the report writer may request a psychiatric report. The pre-sentence report will also deal with the person's physical, or other, ability to carry out work.

If the plea is not guilty the matter is set down for trial. Directions are given that are essentially the timetable for certain events to take place such as the 'service of disclosure' and the response to the (prosecution) 'case statement' by the defence.

The role of the magistrates is that of adjudicator, however, when in the Crown Court the adjudicator role is taken by the jury. The judge meanwhile, oversees the running of the trial and adjudicates on any legal/policy arguments that may arise. If convicted after trial in the Crown Court the judge may sentence immediately if he or she feels that they have sufficient information to do so they may adjourn for a pre-sentence report.

Turning back to our case of R v John Smith, John decided to plead not guilty but was convicted after trial. Unknown to us at the start but now disclosed at his sentencing is the fact that John had a number of convictions to his name, two of which were for violent offences. The judge decided that she had sufficient information and powers to sentence John immediately. She sentenced him to 2 years imprisonment, and so John spent his first night, of many to come, living in rent free accommodation courtesy of Her Majesty's Prison Service.

Conclusion

In this chapter we have walked with John as he has travelled through the criminal justice system and felt criminal procedure in action. He has been arrested and interviewed in accordance with Police And Criminal Evidence act (PACE) requirements which also saw that his treatment whilst in custody complied with criminal procedure as set out in PACE. John was released on conditional bail and duly surrendered on time to be charged with an offence. John then appeared in court and saw the machinery of justice in full swing at both his court appearances and felt the criminal procedure control the processes that governed his journey through his court appearances and sentencing.

Chapter 2 - The civil legal process - **Jon Nicholson**

Introduction

There are many types of civil court proceedings, including commercial disputes for alleged breaches of contract, libel cases and challenges to the decisions of public bodies, to name but a few. However, most civil cases involving expert psychiatrists will be claims for damages for personal injury or clinical negligence and this chapter will therefore focus on those specific areas. Much (but not all) of what is written here will be equally true of other types of civil litigation.

Since 1999, the practice of civil litigation has been governed by the Civil Procedure Rules, often abbreviated to CPR. The person bringing the claim is referred to as the claimant. Before the introduction of the CPR, they were called the plaintiff and this term is still used in other countries. The person against whom the claim is brought has always been known as the defendant.

The CPR is divided into various chapters or 'parts'. Each part has an accompanying "Practice Direction". There are also various protocols. Part 35 of the CPR and accompanying

Practice Direction deal with expert evidence. There is also a "protocol for the instruction of experts to give evidence in civil claims". These documents are easily located online and are essential reading for any psychiatrist intending to give expert evidence for a civil claim.

The relevant law

Most personal injury claims involve the law of negligence and, by definition all clinical negligence claims do so. Lawyers often say there are four components to establishing liability in a negligence claim: duty, breach, causation and damage.

The first component is that the claimant must prove that the defendant owed a 'duty of care'. This is the duty which, for example, a motorist owes other road users not to cause them injury through negligent driving, or which doctors owe their patients to exercise appropriate professional care and skill in their treatment. It is a duty to take reasonable care.

The claimant must then show that this duty has been breached. This means that the claimant must prove that the defendant failed to take reasonable care. This is often referred to simply as 'negligence'. In a clinical negligence claim against a psychiatrist, a psychiatric expert may be asked to give an opinion on whether the defendant was negligent. It is long established that in such a case the question is whether a reasonably competent medical practitioner in the relevant specialism at that time, faced with the same situation, would have responded in the same way. It is a defence to a claim for clinical negligence if there was a body of reasonable and respected medical opinion that would have treated in the same way, even if they are a minority, provided that such an approach had some logical basis. This is known as the 'Bolam test' (after the case in which it was first formulated).

The next stage is for the claimant to show that the negligence caused the injury or damage for which the claim is being made. This is known as 'causation'. Compensation is only payable if causation is established. This can sometimes be a difficult area if the injury is a medical condition, which in fact, has multiple causes. he test is whether the injury would probably have been avoided 'but for' the negligence.

Finally, the claimant must show damage. Such damage may be an injury and its financial consequences. In personal injury claims, this may be the only area in which the expert psychiatrist is involved. The expert may be asked to give an opinion on the condition and prognosis for a psychiatric injury (and perhaps to confirm that this was probably caused by the alleged negligence).

The burden is on the claimant to prove his or her case. The standard of proof required is known as the 'balance of probabilities'. This means that the claimant only needs to show that it is more likely than not that the defendant was negligent and that this caused the injury complained of. It is not necessary to prove these matters 'beyond reasonable doubt' (as in criminal cases). It is also not necessary to apply scientific standards of proof. This is an area which often causes medical experts some difficulty, because of their scientific background and training.

Pre-action protocols

The Civil Procedure Rules include pre-action protocols which govern the behaviour of the parties before proceedings are started at court. There are separate and quite different protocols for personal injury claims and clinical negligence claims.

In a personal injury claim, one of the first steps taken by the claimant is to send a 'letter of claim' to the defendant or their insurers. This letter gives brief details of the accident and the injury and states why the defendant is considered liable. If the claimant is intending to obtain a medical report, he or she will nominate a number of possible experts, normally more than one in each discipline. The letter encloses details of the experts nominated, normally in the form of a curriculum vitae (CV). The defendant then has an opportunity to object to one of more of the nominated experts. The claimant should then obtain a report from an expert to whom the defendant has not objected. For this purpose, expert psychiatrists may be asked to produce abbreviated CVs and details of how their work is divided between claimants and defendants (which appears to be the main criterion used by defendants when deciding whether to object).

In a clinical negligence claim, the experts are instructed before the letter of claim is drafted. This is because the claimant will normally need expert evidence in order to establish whether there is a claim and, if so, what the precise allegations are. There is no opportunity for the defendant to object to the claimant's choice of expert in a clinical negligence claim. Once the necessary expert evidence has been obtained, the claimant will then send a detailed letter of claim setting out the allegations of clinical negligence. Although the clinical negligence letter of claim will be based on an expert's opinion about the standard of care, that report is not normally disclosed until much later in the process.

In both types of case, the defendant has to write a 'letter of response' stating whether liability is admitted or denied. If liability is denied, reasons must be given. The deadline for the letter of response is 3 months in a personal injury claim and 4 months in a clinical negligence claim. In clinical negligence cases, defendants often require more than 4 months to obtain their own expert evidence on the allegations.

If the letter of response admits liability, then the parties may then negotiate a settlement, without the need to involve the court. If liability is denied and the claimant is not persuaded by the reasons given for this, then the next step is to issue court proceedings. Such proceedings may also be issued in cases where liability is admitted, but the parties are unable to agree on the amount of compensation payable.

The stages of a civil claim

Personal injury and clinical negligence claims are issued in a local County Court or in the Queen's Bench Division of the High Court, depending on value. The Central Office of the High Court is based at the Royal Courts of Justice in London, but there are also branches throughout the country, known as District Registries.

The claimant issues a 'claim form' (previously known as a writ) and sends this to the defendant. The claim form will be accompanied by the following documents:-

1. The 'particulars of claim', which is a formal 'statement of case' or 'pleading', setting out the claimant's allegations in detail. In a clinical negligence case against a psychiatrist, the claimant's psychiatric expert will be asked to approve this document.

2. Medical reports dealing with the claimant's condition and prognosis in respect of the injuries for which compensation is sought. If this includes a psychiatric injury, then there should be a condition and prognosis report from a psychiatrist. In a clinical negligence

claim, these reports only deal with condition and prognosis. Opinions on negligence are not disclosed at this stage.

3. A separate schedule setting out the financial losses claimed (such as loss of earnings and the cost of treatment).

The defendant must then serve a 'defence'. This is another formal statement of case setting out the defendant's response to each of the allegations made in the particulars of claim.

The next stage is for a procedural judge to review the papers and to fix or approve a timetable for the remainder of the litigation. This timetable is known as the 'directions order'. It is usually agreed between the solicitors acting for the claimant and those acting for the defendant. In the absence of agreement, the court will fix the timetable at a hearing known as a 'case management conference' (CMC).

In addition to the timetable, the directions order will deal with permission to rely upon expert evidence. Such evidence can only be relied upon with the permission of the court. The court is under a duty to restrict expert evidence to that which is reasonably required to resolve the issues in the case.

Sometimes the court will direct that experts in a particular discipline are to be jointly instructed by both parties. This occurs where the expert is addressing an issue which is peripheral to the claim as a whole. Psychiatrists will not be jointly instructed to report on breach of duty and causation or on a psychiatric condition which is the main injury for which the claim is made. However, if, for example, a claimant is depressed because of disabilities caused by severe physical injury, it is possible that a psychiatrist will be jointly instructed to address this aspect. Joint experts will receive either an agreed set of joint instructions or a separate letter of instruction from each party. They will then send their report to both parties simultaneously and each party will pay half of their fee.

The first step after the CMC is invariably disclosure of documents. Each side gives the other lists of documents in their possession which are relevant to the issues in the case, but which were not created for the purposes of the case. Documents created for the purposes of the case (such as draft expert reports) are 'privileged' and need not be disclosed.

Usually all of the documents relevant to the expert's psychiatric evidence (principally medical records) will have been obtained and supplied to the expert at a much earlier stage in the case. However, occasionally, further relevant documents come to light at this point and are sent to experts for comment.

The next stage is the exchange of statements of factual witnesses. There is a distinction between factual witnesses and expert witnesses. Witnesses of fact can only give evidence on matters which they saw and observed and are not supposed to offer opinions. Only expert witnesses can give opinion evidence.

The statements of factual witnesses are usually exchanged simultaneously, with each side posting copies of their statements to the other at the same time, so that they cross in the post. If the other side's witness statements contain anything which may be relevant to a psychiatric expert's opinion, then he or she should to be sent copies of those statements. This will invariably be the case in a clinical negligence claim involving allegations against a treating psychiatrist, because that psychiatrist will have produced a statement explaining his or her actions.

In cases where both parties have instructed experts in the same field, the next stage is the exchange of the reports of any expert witnesses dealing with issues relevant to establishing liability. In most personal injury claims, there is no expert evidence on liability but such evidence is invariably required in clinical negligence cases where breach of duty or causation is disputed.

A psychiatrist who is giving expert evidence on liability in a clinical negligence claim will normally be asked to review his or her report before exchange. This is an opportunity for the report to be finalised to take into account the opposing party's statement of case, witness statements and any further documents which have come to light. The reports are then exchanged simultaneously in the post, in the same way as witness statements.

After the exchange of expert evidence, the next stage is for the opposing experts in each discipline to discuss the case and to prepare a joint statement setting out the relevant issues upon which they agree and those upon which they disagree and why. These discussions take place between the experts alone, often by telephone, without lawyers present. In clinical negligence cases, the parties' legal representatives will normally provide an agreed set of agenda questions to assist the experts in ensuring that their joint statement addresses all of the relevant issues. However, an agenda is unlikely to be provided in a straightforward personal injury claim.

It is important that experts understand that the purpose of the discussion is not for them to compromise their views in the interests of saving court time. The purpose is to identify the genuine areas of agreement and disagreement. Such discussions are considered in more detail in Chapter 14.

The vast majority of civil cases are settled before trial and 'out of court'. Before the introduction of the CPR, such settlements often occurred at the very last minute or 'at the doors of the court'. This still happens, but is now much less common. Settlements can occur at any stage during the litigation process.

The vast majority of civil trials are conducted by a judge without a jury. The parties are normally represented by barristers, rather than solicitors. The solicitor's role is to prepare the case and to assemble the evidence. Barristers are trial specialists who present cases in court and who advise on how a judge is likely to respond to the evidence. If an expert is giving evidence at trial, it is likely that he or she will have been introduced to the barrister beforehand. A meeting with a barrister is referred to as a 'conference'. In clinical negligence cases and other complex matters there may be a number of conferences before trial.

The procedure at trial is that the claimant's barrister introduces the case to the judge. Evidence is then given by the factual and expert witnesses, who may be asked questions by both barristers and by the judge. Both barristers then give speeches seeking to persuade the judge that their client should win. The judge will then make a decision. Sometimes this is a verbal judgment which is delivered almost immediately. In other cases, judgment may be "reserved" and the judge will produce a written document weeks or months later analysing the evidence and reaching a conclusion.

It is not normally necessary for an expert witness to be at court throughout the trial. However, it may be helpful for them to hear factual witness evidence which is relevant to their opinion. The expert witness will also be expected to be at court whilst the opposing expert is giving evidence, so as to assist the barrister in the cross-examination of that expert. Chapter 15 deals with giving evidence at trial.

Written questions to experts

The CPR allows a party to write directly to an opposing expert with questions to be answered. This can happen at two stages: before proceedings and after proceedings.

After proceedings, such questions can be put once only, within 28 days of receipt of the report, and only for the purposes of clarification of the report. These restrictions do not apply to questions put under the personal injury pre-action protocol prior to the issue of proceedings. The fee for answering opposing questions put before the issue of proceedings should be paid by the questioner. After issue, the fee is payable by the instructing party (presumably on the basis that the party who serves the report which is unclear should bear the cost of clarification).

Although questions can be sent direct to the opposing expert, they should also be copied to the instructing solicitor. An expert who receives such questions should discuss them with the instructing solicitor to check that the questions are proper and have been asked within the required timescale. It is also prudent to check that both sides agree on who is paying the fee. The answers to the questions must be the expert's own independent professional opinion, but there is no difficulty with discussing draft answers with the instructing solicitor before these are finalised.

Legal costs

Until very recently, the normal rule in civil cases was that the loser pays the winner's reasonable legal costs, including expert fees. This has now changed for personal injury and clinical negligence cases, so that most unsuccessful claimants no longer have to pay the defendant's legal costs, but this can still happen in some circumstances.

In theory, this does not affect the expert psychiatrist, because the expert's contract is with the solicitor who instructed him or her and that solicitor must pay the agreed fee irrespective of whether that fee is then recovered from the opposing party. However, it is helpful for experts to have an understanding of legal costs, particularly if they are instructed by claimants.

If the losing party is required to pay the winner's legal costs, then they only have to pay reasonable costs, including reasonable expert fees. If there is no agreement about the amount of legal costs to be paid, then this is decided by the court at a separate hearing, called a 'detailed assessment hearing'. Such hearings are rare, because costs are normally agreed. However, any agreement will depend on what the parties believe a Costs Judge would probably decide at a detailed assessment hearing.

The Costs Judge will assess the reasonableness of an expert's fees by looking at two factors: the hourly rate and the time spent. The Costs Judge will consider whether the hourly rate is in line with that charged by other experts in the same field and whether the time spent appears reasonable in the light of the complexity of the issues, volume of documents etc. Experts will therefore find that they will be asked to break down their invoices in this way and solicitors may also ask for an explanation as to why a piece of work took as long as it did.

Of course, the expert will (or should) have been paid long before any detailed assessment hearing. Any decision by a Costs Judge about the reasonableness of the expert's fee does not affect the solicitor's liability to pay the expert the fee which has been agreed. However, experts are able to earn the goodwill of their instructing solicitors by providing information to assist in the recovery of their fees.

Many personal injury and clinical negligence claims are brought on the basis of 'no win, no fee'. This means that the claimant's solicitor is relying upon winning the case and recovering the legal costs from the unsuccessful defendant in order to be paid. As a consequence, most claimants' solicitors do not receive any money for legal costs until the end of the case. This puts a strain on their cash flow and they may therefore ask experts to agree to defer payment of their fee until the end of the case.

Obviously, experts cannot accept instructions on a 'no win, no fee' basis, because this would compromise their independence (and is expressly forbidden in the CPR). However, there is no ethical or legal objection to an expert offering extended credit or even agreeing to wait until the end of the case before being paid, as long as payment is made irrespective of the outcome. Whether an expert chooses to offer such payment terms is entirely an economic decision for him or her. Doing so is likely to increase the number of instructions received.

Medical reporting agencies exist as an alternative solution to this problem. Such agencies offer experts a volume of work in exchange for the expert agreeing a fee which is significantly lower than would normally be charged. The solicitor who commissioned the report then pays the agency the much higher 'normal' fee, in exchange for an extended period of credit. Many solicitors and experts do not enjoy working with medical reporting agencies but they exist because of the difficulty which claimant solicitors have in paying experts promptly when they themselves are not going to be paid until the end of the case.

The legal costs payable by defendants are said to be unacceptably high and reforms have recently been implemented to try and reduce these. These measures include requiring courts to consider the cost of an expert before deciding whether to give permission to rely upon his or her evidence. Parties to civil litigation are also required to produce detailed budgets setting out their anticipated costs, including expert fees, so that the court can control this. For both of these reasons, experts will increasingly be asked to give detailed estimates of their fees not only for the initial report, but also for their subsequent involvement in the case, possibly up until trial. The more experienced the expert, the more accurate such an estimate is likely to be. Less experienced experts may benefit from discussing these issues with a colleague or with their instructing solicitor.

Chapter 3 - The family legal process - **Nadia Salam**

Types of courts

In England and Wales there are a number of different courts. Family law matters are dealt with in the Family Division of the High Court, by District Judges in County Courts, and in Family Proceedings Courts, which are specialist Magistrates' Courts. The procedures in the Family Proceedings Court are very different from the criminal courts.

In the Family Proceedings Court (FPC) there are often lay magistrates referred to as Justices of the Peace (or JPs). There are usually three Magistrates that sit together and they are collectively called 'the bench'. Magistrates are not legally qualified and are typically part time; they are assisted by a Legal Advisor who will sit in court with them; the Legal Advisor's role is to advise the bench about the law before they make a decision. You can also have a District Judge sitting alone in the FPC.

In the County Court there is usually a District Judge or a Circuit Judge. A Judge in the County Court has greater powers in family cases than a Judge or Magistrate in the FPC.

A Circuit Judge is more senior than a District Judge, a Deputy District Judge is the name for a part time District Judge.

Types of cases

There are a number of different types of cases that the family courts deal with. They can be broadly divided into the following:

- Private child law (this is where there are often parental disputes over the upbringing of the children)
- Public child law (this is where local authority intervention is needed for child protection matters)
- Divorce and Civil Partnerships decrees, including financial remedies
- Financial support for children
- Domestic abuse
- Adoption

CAFCASS in children cases

In private child law and public child law the Children and Families Court Advisory and Support Service (CAFCASS) provides officers (usually trained social workers by profession) to advise the court about what is in the best interests of the children who are subject to the case. CAFCASS is independent of social services and is a non-departmental public body.

In private child law matters where there are disputes between the parents the court may ask CAFCASS to write a report or carry out other work to help the family or to help the court reach a decision. In private child law matters which are complex the court may ask CAFCASS to appoint an officer to act as a Guardian for the child.

In public child law matters where the local authority wants to take the children into care, CAFCASS are always asked to provide a Guardian for the child. The Guardian will be involved throughout the case and will be asked to advise the Court on what is in the best interests of the child, and whether or not the local authority plans for the child are right for the child.

Where the CAFCASS officer is appointed a Guardian, they will also have a solicitor acting on their behalf in addition to the other parties in the case.

Law

In England and Wales there are three main types of law; they set out what can and cannot be done:

- Acts of Parliament referred to as statutes or primary legislation
- Secondary or delegated legalisation, the main type being Statutory Instruments
- Common law, this is not created by Parliament but by Judges in the form of their judgements in cases

The courts generally have only the powers specifically given to them by Parliament through statute. The Magistrates Court Act 1980 and the Superior Courts Act 1981 broadly tells judges what they can and cannot do. In a limited category of cases a High Court Judge has additional powers which are referred to as 'Inherent Jurisdiction'; this is because they have the power to make orders that are not specially contained in any Act of Parliament.

There are a number of key statutes that cover aspect of family law. The main statute for both private and public child law is

The Children Act 1989. Other key statutes used in family law matters are:

- The Matrimonial Causes Act 1973
- The Inheritance (Provisions for Family and Dependents) Act 1973
- The Child Abduction & Custody Act 1985
- The Family Law Act 1986
- The Child Support Act 1991
- The Family Law Act 1996
- The Trusts of Land and Appointment of Trustees Act 1996
- The Protection from Harassment Act 1997
- The Human Rights Act 1998
- The Adoption and Children Act 2002
- The Mental Capacity Act 2005
- The Civil Partnership Act 2004

Family Procedure Rules

In addition to the statutes listed above, the Family Procedure Rules 2010 (FPR) contain the court rules. Court rules are revised frequently; it is therefore important to check that your copy of the rules is up to date. The most recent version can be found on the Ministry of Justice website.

There are some sections of the FPR that say the Civil Procedure Rules (CPR) apply. The CPR are mainly non-family rules. These can also be found on the Ministry of Justice website. Both sets of rules also have Practice Directions which should also be followed.

The expert's duties

The expert's duties can be found in Part 25 FPR. It is important that, as an expert, you familiarise yourself with Part 25 and the related Practice Directions.

The expert's primary duty is to the court, and to assist the court with matters within their expertise. This duty overrides any obligation to the person who pays or instructs the expert. The expert's duty is also to answer the questions about which the expert is required to give an opinion; the expert is to provide that opinion independent of the party, or parties, instructing the expert.

Instructing experts

In family proceedings, an expert cannot be instructed without permission from the court. Parties must apply for permission to instruct an expert at the first available opportunity. The court has the power to restrict expert evidence. In children proceedings, the court will have regard to a number of factors before deciding whether permission should be given to instruct an expert. The factors include:

- any impact on the welfare of the children concerned should permission be given
- the issues to which the expert evidence would relate
- the questions which the court would require the expert to answer
- what other expert evidence is available already obtained
- whether evidence could be given by another person on the matters on which the expert would give evidence
- the impact which giving permission would be likely to have on the timetable, duration and conduct of the proceedings
- the cost of the expert evidence

The factors that the court considers when deciding whether permission should be given in other family proceedings (not children proceedings) are similar. They include:

- the issues to which the expert evidence would relate
- the questions which the court would require the expert to answer
- the impact which giving permission would be likely to have on the timetable, duration and conduct of the proceedings
- the cost of the expert evidence.

If two or more parties wish to put expert evidence before the court on a particular issue, the court may direct that the evidence be given by a single joint expert. The use of a single joint expert is encouraged for a number of reasons, which lead back to the issues the court considers before granting permission to instruct an expert. Where parties cannot agree on the single joint expert the court may select the expert from those identified by the parties.

Often the letter of instruction to the expert will be prepared by one party, unless it is a joint instruction with the other party. It is good practice to have the letter of instruction agreed between all of the parties; where this cannot be done it will usually state this on the letter of instruction. The expert should not have secret conversations with any of the parties; any conversations or communications should be shared.

The expert's report

An expert's report must comply with the requirements set out in Practice Direction 25B FPR in family proceedings. At the end of an expert's report there must be a statement that the expert understands and has complied with the expert's duty to the court.

The expert's report shall be addressed to the court and prepared and filed on time as directed by the court. The report should give details of the expert's qualifications and experience. The report should include a statement identifying the documents contained with the instructions and the substance of any oral instructions, as far as is necessary to explain any opinion or conclusion expressed in the report. The report should also state who carried out any test, examination or interview that has been used for the report, and give details of the qualifications of that person.

The expert should confine the opinion to matters material to the issues in the case and in relation only to the questions that are within the expert's expertise, skill and experience. Where a question has been asked in the letter of instruction that falls outside of the expert's expertise, the expert should state this at the earliest opportunity and volunteer an opinion as to whether another expert is required to bring expertise not possessed by those already involved. The expert in expressing an opinion, should take into consideration all of the material facts including any relevant factors arising from ethnic, cultural, religious or linguistic contexts at the time the opinion is expressed

The evidence should be verified by a statement of truth in the following form:

'I confirm that I have made clear which facts and matters referred to in this report are within my own knowledge and which are not. Those that are within my own knowledge I confirm to be true. The opinions I have expressed represent my true and complete professional opinions on the matters to which they refer.'

Giving evidence at court

Where the court has directed the attendance of an expert witness, the party responsible for the instruction of the expert shall, prior to the hearing at which the expert is to give oral evidence, provide details of the date and time. If the expert's oral evidence is not required then the expert should be notified as soon as possible. Parties should give a logical sequence to the evidence, arranged, where possible, with experts of the same discipline giving evidence on the same day.

If the evidence is being disputed by the parties then they may cross-examine the expert at court to clarify the facts of the disputed matter. Family cases, in particular children cases, are heard in private. Members of the public are not allowed to watch hearings in the same way that is allowed for other areas of law such as criminal law.

Payment of expert fees

The court may give directions about the payment of the expert's fees and expenses and could also limit the amount that can be paid by way of fees and expenses to the expert. Unless the court directs otherwise, the relevant instructing parties are jointly and severally liable for the payment of the expert's fees and expenses.

Where the parties are publically funded by the Legal Aid Agency there will often be a prescribed list of rates for certain experts; the Legal Aid Agency will not pay for any work outside of the rates unless there has been prior approval, which the instructing solicitors will need to request.

Chapter 4 - Medical notes - **Ali Malsher**

The importance of records in a case which has a medico-legal element cannot be underestimated. This is particularly the case where there may be previous entries which are, or are deemed to have relevance to the claim, however tenuous. Of all the medical areas, psychiatric reports rely heavily on detailed examinations of the client, but sometimes appear to be purely an account of a lengthy interview.

However, it is amazing how a small entry in the GP records from 15 years previously, suddenly takes on an importance all on its own once the matter goes to trial. A broad brush approach to medical records might work at an early stage in the case, but certainly will not work if the matter is disputed, the value is significant or the client has a number of difficulties. Put simply therefore, there is no way of avoiding a thorough review of the medical records.

An expert should always work on the basis that the case could go to trial. Few civil cases do; a greater proportion goes to joint expert statements (particularly in clinical negligence) and many settle with one report from a single expert. However, the one occasion an expert is less thorough may also be the one when the lawyer is not on the ball, the client is a poor historian and the other party seeks to challenge the case. The unwritten rule of litigation, whether criminal or civil, is that things tend to go wrong in just the one case rather than spreading the misery throughout the case load. It will always be the case in which an expert has done the least thorough job because everyone thought it would be resolved at the outset.

The first problem for an expert is whether there are any records which can be reviewed and/or whether they are actually in a useable format. Solicitors get records from all types of institutions and most Trusts seem to have had a party with them before they are crammed unceremoniously into an envelope.

Particularly in the field of personal injury, where there are sometimes substantial caseloads of fairly small value claims, lawyers sometimes do not have much time to deal with records. If an expert is dealing with a criminal matter he or she should be aware that most criminal lawyers, even senior ones, can have a surprising ignorance of medical issues.

An expert is more likely to get a copy of what the lawyers get, in the same form they get it. In any case where it is sufficient to justify a conference, consider requesting a fully sorted and paginated bundle. This may not be a popular request but will help everyone at the end (and is work which can be outsourced to specialist agencies).

In addition, records will arrive having been copied somewhat haphazardly in the Trust, followed by being copied quickly in the solicitor's office. The one entry needed will be at the edge of a page and some of it will be missing. It is worth asking the solicitor if their copy has the full entry if it is of relevance. An expert should remember that a solicitor will simply assume all is okay with the records unless they are told otherwise. Ignorance can be peaceful.

The starting point for any review of records is to assume that the legal team, client or judge have little or no knowledge of medical issues. Often that assumption will be entirely correct.

GP records

Quite often GP records form the most important reviews for the psychiatric expert. Unless the client has used the mental health services, the GP records are where small nuggets of information, which may be relevant to the case, are located. GP records are, of course, now mostly computerised (there are still a few surgeries persisting with hand written notes) but the medical records received may not be complete.

GPs tend to use a computer system, the most common of which is EMIS. The EMIS system has a number of different sheets or pages which deal with specific issues. For example there is a prescription page, history page and results pages. There may be a communication page. Quite often busy GP practices simply print off what is the most assessable, which is the list of admissions, entries and attendances at the surgery. It may not, however, list all of the prescriptions.

The correspondence should also be obtained and reviewed. Often, the lengthy letters from hospitals contain useful information for a report. It is worth, therefore, looking through at the outset and checking that the records include everything needed. It takes solicitors a long time to get medical records and it is worth doing the check on receipt.

Never assume that the solicitor has had time to check the records or indeed would have the experience to know that something is missing. Unless an experienced clinical negligence or personal injury solicitor is involved, it is reasonable to assume that little or no checking has been done.

A review of the GP medical records has to indicate significant illnesses or any major procedures. No one is interested in the fractured toe in 1980 but the hysterectomy operation in 2010 should probably be mentioned. As a rule of thumb, if it is thought that the operation or condition is major in the sense that it could, or did, affect the quality of life or psychological health of the client, then it should be mentioned.

Likewise, many conditions may understandably have psychological sequelae which are not obvious at first sight. Tinnitus, vertigo and many other apparently unrelated conditions can lead to depression or anxiety. The lawyers will expect an expert to see past the condition and look at its potential effect on the client.

The volume of records should also be considered, although this is harder to judge with computerised records which can be deceptively brief. If the client appears to have taken up residence in the surgery, in the absence of some condition which requires regular review and control, this should be noted. If the client has attended with many different complaints some of which have not yet been considered by medical science, this is worthy of comment.

The medication regime should be mentioned if appropriate. If the client is simply in possession of an aspirin and the odd course of antibiotics, clearly that is not relevant. If the client is taking the contents of a medicine cabinet on a daily basis then this may be relevant. Many medications have potential psychiatric side effects – steroid psychosis is the most extreme perhaps, but the legal team may not be aware of them.

It goes without saying, that any entry detailing anxiety, stress or tearfulness should be detailed and reviewed. Any reference to counselling should be mentioned and cross checked with any notes that might be available from the counsellors. Until the advent of IAPT (Improving Access to Psychological Therapies) many counsellors were attached to surgeries and their notes may be accessible. It should be borne in mind, however, that counsellors are notorious at not keeping notes or writing them in a form of shorthand that cannot be deciphered, even by a war time code breaker!

Another important aspect, which is often neglected, is the issue of any childhood or adolescent anxieties and psychological problems. Of course, it needs to be borne in mind that the individual may have had an over anxious parent, who sought to take the child to the GP surgery on a regular basis for fairly small matters.   Nevertheless, if there are referrals to child and adolescent mental health service or references to depression, anxiety and so on, these should be mentioned.

Likewise, social services input may be relevant, but an expert should be wary about including too much detail. Letters often find their way into records which are part of family proceedings and non disclosable. Judges can be difficult about recitations of family proceedings for that reason. GPs often accumulate letters from sources which includes information that should not be in the public domain. The fact that it is there, does not necessarily guarantee that detailed reference to it would be considered acceptable.

In the absence of being instructed by a family lawyer, however, do not assume that the legal team understand the disclosure rules of family proceedings.   Civil lawyers, in particular, can be cavalier about disclosure and assume the same applies in other areas of law. Family lawyers are quite the opposite.

The older Lloyd George records are often incomprehensible and will never be in any logical date order. If there are words of relevance that can be deciphered mention them - even if it is not possible to identify exactly what proceeds or follows the entry.

Hospital records

Hospital records generally come in a number of different sections, namely correspondence, clinical, operative, results, nursing, charts and physiotherapy.

In a sizeable minority of cases the only hospital records you may receive are in relation to their attendance at the Accident & Emergency Department. Emergency department records are fairly limited, but where an admission follows the attendance, there is likely to be a full

medical clerking. This is often undertaken by the most junior of the medical hierarchy, more likely to be legible and detailed in approach.

These records are also notorious for missing anything psychological or psychiatric. They tend to concentrate on the body systems and investigations. There may be a cursory mention of an obvious psychological or psychiatric issue, but short of a patient holding a suicide note and a basket of tablets, this is mostly missing.

The A & E records, however, should have a list of previous attendances though not usually the reasons. Again, a person who has seemingly 'moved into' the department might be worth a mention but if their leisure activities are boxing and rugby that may be of less significance.

The correspondence should be reviewed. It does not need to be reviewed in any detail if, for example, it relates simply to surgical procedures and clinic appointments. As with the GP records, if the correspondence notes medication or treatment that could, or did, have an effect on the mental health of the client, it should be mentioned.

References to any vulnerability should be considered. It may be perfectly logical that the client is tearful following her husband being diagnosed with terminal cancer or less so that she reacts in the same way when told she has a minor soft tissue injury. Either way it should be mentioned, although placing it in context is important.

Clinical records follow the standard pattern - clerking, less detailed review by the more senior members of the team and ward round scribbles. Again most of these records are unlikely to be of importance to the psychiatric review. However, it is always worth working through the clinical notes just to check whether there are entries from the on-call psychiatric team whilst the client was an inpatient. Most of these are easily understood by fellow medics, but please note that abbreviations change and increase as new investigations or procedures develop and may need 'translation'.

A psychiatric expert is not expected to do a detailed analysis of operative procedures, investigations, charts and outpatient appointments unless relating to mental health. However, they are expected to pick up every issue which may be possibly construed as indicating a psychiatric vulnerability (however tenuous) and any other issue which may relate to mental health. Some of these may be stretching reality somewhat but it is better to include than to ignore these. In essence, if a member of the mental health services has walked anywhere near the client and made an entry in the medical records, this should be noted in detail.

If there is an issue about behaviour on the ward or within the hospital environment the nursing 'Kardex' will provide details. In any event, for a psychiatric expert the most helpful records are often those of the nurses and physiotherapists. Both tend to write more detailed holistic views of the patient than those found in the clinical records, which can be brief updates on physical condition alone.

The nursing 'Kardex' generally includes a fairly standard care plan, daily account and communication sheets. The care plans themselves tend to be of little assistance, since they generally follow a standard type of wording. The daily 'Kardex' which records the condition of the client, however, may be much more detailed. Sometimes the information is separated into different problems, so psychological issues may appear not only under anxiety but perhaps also under pain control. Of course the person in pain may have a valid reason for their distress, but not if all they require is paracetamol once a day.

Nursing records are generally in narrative form. The daily 'Kardex' is like a diary account of events. Sometimes they are informative to the point of tedium, sometimes ridiculously brief. However most records fall somewhere between the two. Unlike clinical notes, nurses tend to write records other people can read. This is a huge advantage.

Most nursing records include a communication sheet, which details appointments and meetings. They will also include discussions with the family or sometimes with the individual themself. Often these can be a valuable source of information. Nursing records are sometimes written within the clinical records, as a separate set of records or as a mixture of the two. For example, the ward nurse may have a separate 'Kardex' whilst the tissue viability nurse or the diabetic nurse may write in the clinical records in the same way as a visiting medic might do.

The other notes which may be helpful are those of the physiotherapists, who often have a separate collection of notes which find their way eventually into the main records. Physiotherapists have their own system of abbreviations and hieroglyphics which defeat even the most hardened translator of medical records, but they also include references to how the patient is emotionally. The medical and surgical issues will not be unfamiliar to a psychiatric expert, even if it is ten years since they attended a medical or surgical ward. What the court wants is someone to pick out the entries (if any) which suggest a vulnerability, or causally link events and conditions. The context of an individual presenting with psychiatric problems is as important as the degree to which he or she may be affected. These are issues which may seem obvious to the expert but will not necessarily be detected by the legal team, and will not be considered by the judge at all, unless it is pointed out to him.

If all else fails, an expert should also be aware that all lawyers are impressed by long documents, even if some of their content is irrelevant. There is less likely to be a criticism of not being thorough or missing elements of the history if the report is full. More importantly, judges feel that an expert has done his or her job if there is a detailed chronology, even if most of the entries are of little relevance. On a practical basis, if the case gets to court, cross examination is less likely on the omissions of a report if there aren't any!

Chapter 5 - Things to avoid in an expert report - Cyrene Aboy

By the time you reach this chapter, you will have gained an appreciation of the key role your medical report will play in the legal proceedings. Sometimes you will receive instructions to prepare a report from a medical agency used by the instructing solicitors; this is most common in personal injury cases. At other times and for other types of report you may receive instructions directly from the solicitor. For the purposes of this chapter I am going to concentrate on personal injury cases.

Letter of instruction

The letter of instruction can come in different formats, but it should, at the very least, provide you with the following:

1. Basic personal and contact details of the person you are required to examine
2. Accident/incident circumstances
3. The injuries sustained and ongoing problems
4. The questions or areas you are required to explore when preparing your report

5. A list of any attachments or medical records you are required to consider

6. Details of who will be paying your invoice

7. A reiteration of your duty under the relevant protocol and your paramount duty to the court

The letter of instruction will usually have been drafted by the person with conduct of the case, who may have devoted considerable time to drafting this tailor-made letter to you. Whilst the introductory paragraphs may appear exactly identical from one letter of instruction to another, it is important that you actually take time to read the instructions and familiarise yourself with the issues you are specifically asked to explore in your report. A good medico-legal report will address the issues specifically raised in the instructions by weaving it, seamlessly and methodically, into the relevant parts of the report.

There are two mistakes that you should try to avoid when dealing with the letter of instruction. The first mistake is not reading it thoroughly, and the second is not checking that all the enclosures mentioned as being attached, are, in fact, present. Making one, or both, these mistakes can lead to your report coming back to you for revision, which creates work that could have been avoided in the first place.

The report itself

The ideal report will be one that has been drafted soon after the examination has taken place and following review of the medical records.

Basic details

A common mistake to make is a failure to check the basic details of the individual you have examined. Getting this seemingly trivial (in the grand scheme of things) detail wrong, on the covering page of your report, does not create a good first impression.

Terminology

You will usually need to use technical medical terms in your report. It is, however, important to remember that your report will be read by non-medical parties who will not be familiar with the day to day terminology that you use in your practice.

Medico-legal reports should explain, either in parentheses in the report itself or in an appendix attached to the end of the report, the terminology, test or assessment scale applied during the examination. Whilst a 'GAF score of 55' may be self-explanatory to you as an expert, legal professionals will find it difficult to appreciate the importance of this if the purpose of the assessment and what the score reveals, is not explained in the report. It is therefore paramount that when you use such terms you do not assume that the instructing party will understand their significance.

Review of the records

The detailed review of the records provided to you, as discussed in detail in the previous chapter, is a basic expectation of instructing parties. No matter how experienced a solicitor is, they will never have the intimate medical knowledge you possess to know something relevant is missing or anomalous from the medical records, as they seldom have the time to review each entry in detail. A casual glance at the records will not suffice and such temptation must be avoided. If, during your diligent review of the records, you identify entries you consider relevant yet very limited in their impact on the live issues, it is best to remark on them, rather than avoiding mentioning them altogether. A common mistake is presuming that instructing parties are not interested in peripheral issues. The disappointing impression left by a report that fails to discuss the intricacies of relevant medical records remains for an unbelievably long time and may very well influence whether that particular solicitor instructs you again.

Opinion

The expert opinion you express in your report should be clear and unambiguous if possible. If you cannot be certain of an issue, avoid being elusive. It is best to explain why you cannot be more precise rather than providing a vague statement which will only result in the instructing party writing to you asking you to clarify your opinion.

In personal injury claims, your report will be used to determine the appropriate level of compensation depending on the extent of the injuries attributable to the accident. As long as the injuries are more likely than not to be a result of the accident, the injuries sustained will be compensated. Essentially, what the instructing party expects is that you express your opinion on a balance of probabilities. Of course, if you are certain than the psychiatric injury is directly attributable to the accident, then say so, but if you cannot be certain, do not forget that the standard of proof is on a balance of probabilities and not beyond reasonable doubt (the latter being that pertaining in criminal cases).

There will be times when, although you are able to provide an opinion, the opinion of another medical expert might be more suitable. Should you find yourself in this particular situation, it is usually best to declare that, although you have an opinion on the matter, given your expertise and experience of similar cases, the opinion of a specific expert may provide a better insight and view on that particular issue. Having said this, do not forget that instructing parties are relying on your expert recommendation as to whether or not obtaining additional reports is proportionate and/or reasonable. You should, therefore, avoid suggesting the need for further reports from other experts if you do not consider the areas they will address are significant, or relevant, to key aspects of the issues as you see them.

Treatment

In some cases you will be able to comment on any recommended treatment the individual will need as part of their recovery. If treatment sessions are required, you should include an estimated number of sessions and an estimate of the costs if possible (although please note that some agencies positively discourage this as they wish to put forward their own services - if in doubt, always defer to the solicitor). A report that recommends treatment but is silent on the above is likely to result in a further enquiry from the instructing party or the medical agency asking you to clarify your views.

Prognosis

At the end of your report you will be expected to provide a prognosis for any ongoing symptoms. If, in your expert opinion having examined the individual, you are able to do this, please express yourself in clear terms. Whether you time it from the date of the examination or from the date of the accident, the time frame must be clear. A clear prognosis allows legal professionals to value a claim and allows them to discuss with their client the option to settle their claim based on your prognosis, without waiting for its expiry.

If however, you cannot be clear on the prognosis and you feel a re-examination further down the line is necessary (for example if the individual has not recovered and or is engaged in treatment) do not hesitate to say so. A qualified prognosis is better than a long distant prognosis as the progress can be reassessed at a later stage allowing for a more accurate valuation of the injuries sustained. The prognosis period is a key aspect of the compensation assessment carried out by legal professionals; it is therefore important to avoid giving a tenuous prognosis unaccompanied by a recommended point for re-examination.

Questions following the report

Even the most thorough medical report may elicit a question from the instructing party or their opponents. Most of the time, the questioner will ask you to confirm that their understanding of your report is correct, but sometimes the questions will ask (demand) that you pin point with great accuracy the opinions you have expressed. In many cases, it will be difficult to answer the questions any more clearly than you have expressed in your report, so do not feel obliged to expand or develop your opinion for the sake of answering the question. If the examination and the records could not provide you with that degree of clarity at the time of writing your report, there may well be no reason why you would be able to do so at this later stage.

Further reports

In some cases, you will be instructed more than once during the length of a claim. In those cases, it is paramount that you revisit your previous reports to ensure the consistency and cogency of your evidence. It is no exaggeration to say that a contradictory view in a second report from the same expert, with no clear rationale, can break a claim and will often make the instructing party question whether or not they instructed a reliable expert in the first place. Whilst your expert opinion will inevitably change in some circumstances, the substance of your reports should essentially remain the same between your reports. Should you need to revise or contradict an earlier report, do so transparently and do not avoid tackling the issue directly. If there are new factors that have come into play and affected your expert opinion, do not forget to discuss this in your second/addendum report.

Usually, you will find that you are instructed to provide further reports when the claim has been issued at court and there is a court timetable in place. Court directions are now more stringent than ever. It is therefore vital that any court deadlines relating to the submission of your report are adhered to by all involved. If you receive instructions that are not feasible by the set deadline, do not delay informing the instructing party. With the strong and strict case management powers of the courts brought about by the Jackson reforms in 2013, it is vital that instructing solicitors are told from the outset whether or not you will be able to work within the tight timescales set by the courts. Avoid leaving it too late to inform the instructing solicitors as this will not leave them enough time to prepare a successful application to the court to vary the directions timetable.

Joint statements

At the advanced stage of proceedings, and after expert evidence has been exchanged between the parties, you may be required to prepare a joint statement with your expert counterpart. The purpose of the discussions that take place before the joint statement is drafted is to narrow down the points of dispute in your respective reports. There is no requirement that experts should compromise their views, indeed this would be wrong as their role is not to decide the case, but it is important be receptive to what one's opposite number has to say. Experts should avoid approaching this meeting as a confrontation; it is an open dialogue between the experts, a chance to discuss, scrutinise and work together to summarise for the non-experts the agreements and disagreements in your medical opinions.

Conclusion

The mistakes to avoid discussed in this chapter are unlikely to come as a revelation to most experts, but with the number of issues you need to concentrate on in your report, some of these basic requirements can fall by the wayside. Avoiding making these simple mistakes ensures that the effort devoted to your preparation of the report will not have to be repeated and the legal process can proceed to its next stages without unnecessary delays.

Chapter 6 - Boundaries between expert evidence and opinion in family cases - **Vikki Martin**

The 2011 Family Justice Review, identified a 'trend towards an increasing and unjustified use of expert witness reports, with consequent delay for children'. As a result of the review, expert evidence must now be deemed 'necessary', allowing judges ruling in family court proceedings to limit the number of expert witnesses who give evidence. Previously, evidence from experts, including psychologists and doctors, was permitted if it was 'reasonably required'. This is no longer the case and key changes include a list of factors which the court must note when deciding whether to give permission. This includes the impact on the court timetable and the likely cost of the expert evidence. Lord Justice Munby, president of the Family Division of the High Court, said: "There is no question of families being denied the chance to call evidence they need to support their case or being denied a fair hearing, but the new test gives judges more control over expert evidence in family proceedings.

The rule change gives family judges the means to make robust case management decisions to make sure the expert evidence is focused and relevant". So, what is considered to be 'necessary'? Case law tells us that 'necessary' has a meaning lying somewhere between 'indispensable' on the one hand and 'useful', 'reasonable' or 'desirable' on the other hand and has the connotation of the imperative; what is demanded rather than what is merely optional or reasonable or desirable.

Despite these developments, expert witnesses remain an essential part of the legal process in many family law cases, providing both factual and opinion evidence. The aim of this chapter is to identify the differences between factual and opinion evidence and the responsibilities associated with acting as an expert witness. The starting point is to understand that the essential role of a witness is to assist a court's determination of the facts and issues.

The expert evidence considered by the court will include the report (plus an addendum report if necessary) and the attendance of the expert at Court where they can be cross-examined by the advocates and judge. It is essential to remember, as an expert witness, that although you will normally be retained by one of the parties, or more than one of the parties, as a single joint expert, your overriding duty is to the court to provide a competent and impartial opinion, in order to enable the court to discharge its fundamental duty in its final determination of the case to regard the child's welfare as paramount.

Role of the expert

The family courts make crucial decisions that affect the safety and future lives of children and their families. The role of the expert witness is to assist the court by providing advice on matters requiring specialist expertise outside the knowledge of the court. Applications for the appointment of a psychiatrist to undertake a psychiatric assessment are likely to be made where there are concerns raised about a parent's mental health, substance or alcohol misuse, or a potential personality disorder.

This usually requires the parent's consent, unless there is real reason to suspect they may be at risk of harming themselves or another person or the child(ren) or may otherwise impact on the child(ren)'s welfare. Commonly, the parties, through their solicitors, will jointly instruct a psychiatrist, normally at equal cost to them or occasionally at the cost of the Local Authority. The final decision as to whether to order psychiatric assessment however, is made at a judge's discretion. The report must be interpreted by the judge, the parties and their advocates. The report must be clear and avoid jargon and complex language. It is sensible to assume that the reader has no, or very limited, knowledge of the subject.

Experts must provide independent advice that conforms to the best practice of their profession and confine their opinion to matters within their skills and experience. This is verified through a signed statement of truth, and may be tested through cross-examination if they are called to give oral evidence in court.

Requirements of Part 25 Family Procedure Rules 2010

Professional competence does not necessarily guarantee competence as an expert witness. Experts also need to develop their knowledge of the legal framework in which they operate and develop skills in writing reports and presenting evidence in court. The role and obligations of all involved in the instruction, work and evidence of expert witnesses in the family courts are laid out in Part 25 Family Procedure Rules 2010 and supporting Practice Directions so it is essential for the expert to be familiar with these provisions. The rules are very specific about the contents of the letter of instruction that should be sent to the appointed expert which can only help the expert when undertaking their assessment and preparing the report. In addition, the Court will now need to have approved the questions to be put to the expert and approve the letter of instruction.

Where a psychiatrist is instructed as an expert in family proceedings the following standard questions are likely to be posed for consideration in the psychiatric evaluation and subsequent report:

- Does the person being assessed suffer from a mental illness or mental disorder?
- To what extent is it possible that any condition found could affect parenting ability?
- What risks does the condition carry for the children, both in terms of physical risk and the potential for emotional and psychological harm or neglect?
- Is there a potential impact on the child's development (if the expert is a child psychiatrist) and/or the parent's ability to provide consistent care (if the expert is an adult psychiatrist)?
- Is treatment/medication an option and what treatments would the psychiatrist recommend?

- Is the condition manageable?

- To what extent does the psychiatrist believe treatment could be effective and what timescales would they deem 'normal' for treatment of any condition identified?

- What support/treatment services are available?

Assessment of the client

It is expected that the expert should consider the case papers prior to commencing the psychiatric assessment. A good starting point is to refer to the list of essential reading set out in the letter of instruction. It is likely to include a social work chronology, parties' medical records, local authority's initial assessment and police logs for example. It would then be expected that the psychiatric assessment would include one or more face-to-face assessments. It may include tests, which are designed to identify mental illness or personality disorders. An expert should be wary of carrying out their assessment before reading all of the background material. All too often the assessment will be completed and report drafted and when subsequent evidence is provided to the expert an addendum report is required which can often undermine the contents of the original assessment.

It is preferable to indicate to the court that the outstanding information is required before the assessment can be completed rather than be placed under time pressure to prepare the report, only to discover that such outstanding information changes the face of the assessment and perhaps the party who is subject to the assessment has been less than honest in their answers. Of course, perhaps the expert would have changed their assessment and questions had the information been available earlier. There will be far more respect for an expert who identifies the need for outstanding information before they are prepared to undertake their assessment than for one who continues regardless simply due to the time pressures of work and the court timetable.

Drafting the report

When drafting the report, it is important, as an expert, to be clear and precise and answer the questions posed and not to stray outside of the scope of what is required as this will potentially taint the expert advice and not assist the court. That is not to say that as an expert you cannot offer the court some additional information which you consider to be necessary and relevant. Remember that the report needs to be user-friendly as it is intended to assist non-experts in understanding the matter in issue who will not be medically or scientifically trained.

Any technical terms used should be explained; matters of fact should be clearly distinguished from matters of opinion. Expert opinion should always be underpinned by sound argument and evidence. Experts should draw upon their skills, knowledge and experience appropriate to the particular case. However, this does not mean there will never be occasions when the evidence is disputed; indeed, the testing of evidence in court is an important part of the process. It is sensible to bear this in mind throughout the drafting process.

The expert should also remember that their report will be read not only by the judge and lawyers but it will also be read by the parties who are probably the parents. It is good practice to assume that one will be asked to justify anything that one has said or written. In a report one should make a point of providing the reasons for having reached particular conclusions. If there are limitations to the report, either because information was unavailable or insufficient time was available with the parent, then the expert should be honest and state this in the report. Reports prepared for court hearings will inevitably be exposed to the very closest scrutiny, and it is worth being extra careful and cautious when preparing such reports.

Being a witness in court

If you are instructed as an expert in family proceedings you will sometimes be required to attend court as a witness. That is likely to be either at a final hearing, if the matter is contested, or at a finding of fact hearing where there are allegations that are in dispute, such as allegations of domestic violence or allegations of a non-accidental injury to a child.

Before attending court it is essential that the expert re-reads their report so that they are fully familiar with the case. The report is the expert's primary evidence to the court. There is more information about answering questions in court in chapter 15. Each party's legal representative will have the opportunity to put questions to the expert and answers should be directed to the judge or magistrates, not the lawyer who is asking the questions. The witness should answer slowly and clearly as the judge and advocates will want to take notes of the answers. If possible simple language should be used. Where an expert is giving a technical answer or explanation then this should be explained clearly. If an expert either does not know an answer to a question, or more importantly if they feel that it is outside their area of expertise then it is important to say so. Never guess an answer or give an opinion outside your expertise.

For example, an adult psychiatrist may be asked questions about a parent's parenting skills. Clearly this is not within their expertise; the most an adult psychiatrist can do is comment on what impact any mental health diagnosis is likely to have on a person's parenting ability. Experts should always be alert to the possibility of being drawn into giving evidence, or expressing opinions, which are beyond their experience or expertise. There is nothing wrong with deferring to someone better suited to answer a particular point; indeed failure to do so will leave the expert open to challenge in subsequent questioning. Judges and lawyers may have a poor understanding of the different areas of psychiatric expertise. Though it can be difficult for an expert to be assertive, particularly if a relevant expert has not been instructed, he or she must resist the temptation to try to be helpful and have a go at answering the question. It is better to state clearly and unequivocally that it is outside one's area of expertise and/or experience.

When questions are posed specifically in relation to comments in their report, the expert should be 'taken' to that specific place. If this does not occur then one should ask for this to be done. It is perfectly acceptable, indeed a good idea, for the expert to re-read that section before answering the question put to them. Experts should remember that during cross-examination it is perfectly acceptable and entirely normal for leading questions to be posed. There is likely to be at least one advocate in the room whose case is not supported by the report. They, in particular, will want to cast doubt on the validity or accuracy of the report, or a comment in it. If the expert remains confident in what they have said in their report, then this needs to come across in the witness box. The advocate may be trying to lead the expert in a different direction to bring about the possibility of a different conclusion. The judge, or magistrates, may also ask questions either during or at the end of the cross-examination process.

Finding of fact hearings

It is not uncommon for factual disputes between parties to arise within private or public law children proceedings. These usually concern domestic violence or substance misuse. It is important to distinguish between serious allegations which (if true) will have a clear impact on the welfare of the child who is the subject of the proceedings, and the decision about whether the court should make a certain order. This is compared with less serious allegations which may not have any impact on the eventual outcome of the proceedings. It is for the court to decide if a finding of fact hearing is needed, not the parties nor CAFCASS, nor the expert.

Judges are reluctant to order separate fact-finding hearings in all but the most serious of cases. They do not want parties (and the public purse) to incur the cost of lengthy litigation where the outcome, either way, is unlikely to inform the court. Very often this can leave the parties in a position where allegations are left hanging in the background. In private law proceedings, allegations are often resurrected much later on by the party making them as a reason for contact not being allowed to progress as quickly as the other party may wish, or at all.

As an expert, it is always easier to be instructed after a finding of fact hearing has taken place. Once a court has made a finding, the expert can approach the issue on the basis that the allegation has either been proved or disproved. It removes the question mark over the allegations and the expert no longer has to report on the basis of assumptions and give analysis on the one hand, if something happened, and on the other hand, if it did not, i.e. coming to two different conclusions.

However, experts do not always have the benefit of findings having been made when they carry out their assessment and report. This is firstly because finding of fact hearings only take place in a very limited number of cases and secondly, because even when they do, the expert may have been directed to report before that hearing has even taken place. In the case of the latter, the expert may be asked to either file an addendum report on the basis of the outcome of the finding of fact or present evidence to the court as to whether the findings have any impact on their conclusions and if so, what. In reality, an expert is normally preparing a report on the basis of allegations alone and not matters of fact. Even where an expert suggests to the court that a finding of fact hearing would assist or even be essential, the court is not compelled to agree.

Given that finding of fact hearings do not take place in every case and it is, therefore, normal for an expert to find themselves preparing a report on the basis of assumptions, the expert should keep this at the forefront of their mind throughout the report drafting process. If no finding has been made in respect of a particular allegation then the report should not be drafted as though it definitely happened or definitely did not happen. Inevitably the expert will need to consider the two alternatives and if these two alternatives would lead to different conclusions then these should be clearly identified. It would be a mistake to report on the basis of one conclusion only. It may subsequently be proven that the opposite is true and the expert faces the risk that their report would then be undermined.

Fact versus opinion

As we have seen from the previous section, much expert evidence is likely to be based upon opinion rather than fact. Although opinion evidence of lay witnesses is not normally admissible in court, opinion evidence from expert witnesses is. Ordinarily it is the role of the court is to reach conclusions based upon its assessment of the information placed before it. Its factual conclusions will (or should) be based upon the evidence of fact put before it; its legal conclusions will be based on its application of the law to the facts it has found, having regard to the legal arguments put before it by the advocates. Thus a witness of fact should not, under ordinary circumstances, be asked questions which require the witness to venture an opinion on a fact in issue. Nor should the expert offer such answers. However, opinion evidence is required when the court needs additional assistance to form an opinion on, and thereby decide justly, a particular issue which concerns matters of specialised knowledge and expertise. Therefore, the court will accept opinion evidence from an expert where that expert is qualified to give that opinion as a result of their qualifications and experience with a view to assisting the court to decide on that particular issue. The evidence that expert witnesses can give is called 'expert opinion evidence', and this evidence is used and admitted where the court lacks competence due to a lack of necessary expertise.

Experts should remember, when writing their report, that the non-expert reader will not necessarily apply appropriate caution to the expert's opinion. Therefore, it is worth bearing in mind that some readers will take opinion as 'gospel', rather than appreciating the limits of the expert's conclusion. If something is opinion, state it as such, whilst identifying clearly the basis upon which that opinion is based.

The expert should exercise caution not to allow bias to creep into their report. For example, upon reading the medical records or police logs disclosed in the case it may be easy to be led towards a negative conclusion before the assessment process has taken place. Medical records and police logs can, by their very nature, include much negative information. Therefore, although this background information is important and will assist the expert in preparing for their assessment of the party, no conclusions should be drawn on the basis of this evidence alone. Selective extraction of negative information is one of the most common faults in medical reports; vigilance and an open mind are needed to avoid this trap. It is also essential that an expert considers and mentions in a report all relevant material, including that which tends to throw doubt on the expert's conclusion.

Conclusion

The modern guidance on the instruction and role of experts in children cases has evolved recently and no doubt will continue to do so as the Single Family Court is rolled out by 1 April 2014. It will be a learning curve for all involved including judges, barristers, solicitors and the experts themselves. There are some simple rules that experts should follow to ensure that their involvement remains indispensable to the courts:

- Experts should act independently of the parties and the exigencies of the court process
- Experts must express only opinions which they genuinely hold and which are not biased in favour of one particular party
- Experts should not mislead by omissions. They should consider all the material facts in reaching their conclusions, and they must not omit to consider the material facts which could detract from their concluded opinion
- Experts should state the facts or assumptions on which their opinion is based
- If experts look for, and report on, factors which tend to support a particular proposition or case, their report should still provide a straightforward, not a misleading opinion, be objective and not omit factors which do not support their opinion and be properly researched
- Experts should have sufficient practical experience in the area on which they are commenting and should make it clear when a particular question or issue falls outside their area of expertise

It is clear that judges are going to be playing a 'gate keeping' role applying new tests as to whether expert evidence and opinion is necessary. If experts are going to be instructed less then competition for the work will inevitably increase. Therefore, reputation will be everything. An expert can ensure their reputation by taking heed of the above factors. Experts should avoid writing lengthy reports that simply state the 'blindingly obvious'. They have been instructed to bring expertise to the case that is not available through the judge or advocates. The report must be clear, precise and answer the questions posed. Provided these rules are followed and experts continue to evolve and adjust with the progressive family law arena, then they are extremely unlikely to be criticised and will remain a valid and essential part of the court process.

Chapter 7 - The need for balance: how to achieve it - Laura Millman & Katherine Pearce

Part 35 of the Civil Procedure Rules CPR) is the 'go to' section for expert reporting and requirements in civil litigation. The rule itself is clear and self-explanatory, supplemented by Practice Direction 35. What is at the core of this rule and, at the heart of a good expert report, is the concept of balance. Rather than rehearsing the details of the rules here, this chapter intends to set out the key elements and considerations, as we see them, to achieve balance when preparing a report for the court:

Procedure

Further to the Supreme Court's decision in *Jones* v *Kaney (2011)*, procedure has never been more important for an expert witness. At risk of teaching you to suck eggs, one of the most important points to keep in mind when preparing your report is your duty - which is to the court and not to your instructing solicitor or their client. It seems so obvious but it can often be overlooked, or indeed forgotten, during the course of your involvement with a claim.

With this duty in mind, and having set out a chronology and summary of the relevant evidence, you should clearly set out the matters which are material in the case and comment on those which are within your expertise. You should quote the questions or allegations plainly, helping you to confine your report to the scope of your instructions, and then provide your opinion on each issue separately.

You will need to state the facts on which your opinion is based and ensure that you distinguish between facts that you know to be true and facts which are assumptions. It is helpful to remember that facts can be disputed and if so, it is for the court to decide which version of the facts they prefer. You should, however, give an explanation as to why you favour one version over another.

You will undoubtedly be faced with cases where there are competing diagnoses and/or situations where there is a range of possible opinions. You will need to clearly set out the competing options in your report, advise of your own opinion and provide evidence, on the balance of probabilities, as to why you favour your opinion over the others. This is a fundamental requirement to achieve a balanced report.

During your consideration of the evidence and the preparation of your report, you may find that you have issues or doubts about the case. Whether those doubts relate to the facts or to your own assumptions based on the documentation considered, you should discuss your concerns with your instructing solicitor by email, letter or telephone call. Your report will be used to assess the strength and weakness of the claim. Remember that lawyers are not medically trained and it may be that something you raise is critical to the legal assessment of the case.

Clinical judgement

Whilst your clinical judgement is critical, clinical judgement alone is not enough. You will need to be clear on your assessment of symptom validity and include in your report objective measurements or corroboration with other sources of information to back up your opinion. You need to justify why you have reached the conclusion you have, with reference to the evidence in the case, your own specialist knowledge and any published references you have relied upon.

We have found it helpful, and indeed it forms part of a court direction in the lead up to trial, that you prepare a literature review containing published sources upon which you intend to rely. Your instructing solicitor is unlikely to be medically trained or qualified. A literature review provides valuable context at this early stage to enable them to understand the basis on which you have come to your opinion.

We have commented on the need to address competing opinions above, but it is critical that, when there is evidence which undermines your opinion, you outline that evidence, be it published reference material or otherwise, and explain clearly why it is not persuasive in this case.

Remember that you are the expert and it is your opinion that is central to the report. Ensure, therefore, that you set out your opinion clearly and succinctly, providing literature references to back it up.

Language and the legal test

When preparing a medico-legal expert report, it is critical to remind yourself of the legal test itself, be it breach of duty, causation, or both, and the language of those tests. The legal test should be clearly set out in the formal instructions from your instructing solicitor, but for ease of reference:

Breach of duty

The case *Bolam v Friern Hospital Management Committee (1957)* established the rule for assessing the appropriate standard of care in cases involving skilled professionals. The Bolam test advises that *"a doctor is not guilty of negligence if he has acted in accordance with a practice accepted as proper by a responsible body of medical men skilled in that particular art…"*

Putting it another way, a doctor is not negligent if he is acting in accordance with a certain practice just because there is a body of opinion which takes a contrary view. The claimant therefore must prove that no responsible body of medical practitioners would have acted as the defendant did. The only modification to the *Bolam* test is in the case of *Bolitho v City & Hackney Health Authority (1997)* where the House of Lords advised that if the body of expert evidence for the defendant cannot be withstand logical analysis, the court would be entitled not to use it as a bench mark.

Causation

In respect of causation, the following question needs to be asked, 'but for the negligence, would the claimant have suffered the damage of which he or she now complains?' (the 'but for' test). Once this has been considered, you will then need to consider whether the breach of duty caused or materially contributed to the damage - what difference, if any, did the breach make to the outcome and would the claimant has suffered the same outcome in any event? You may also be asked to consider factual causation – what would or should have happened but for the breach of duty.

Any causation argument needs to be proven on the balance of probabilities. This means that we can plead as a certainly what can be proved only as a probability. In other words, lawyers do not look for scientific certainty; if a particular outcome would *probably* have been avoided had the negligent act not occurred, then we can plead that that outcome *would* have been avoided. This is what is meant by proving 'on the balance of probabilities' - the likelihood of avoiding the injury is 51% or more. This is a lower threshold than the criminal test of 'beyond a reasonable doubt'.

Having established whether you are reporting on breach, causation or both, read your instructions carefully and make sure you are clear about both the legal test and to the remit of your report to the court. Address each question of allegation of negligence separately.

It is essential that when you are referring to breach of duty you use the language of the legal test - that no responsible body of medical practitioners would have done what was done in this case. By way of example, we have come across an expert advising on breach where the word 'most practitioners' was used. Ask yourself what that means? On cross examination, does this mean that there are some responsible psychiatrists who would have done differently? You can see the difficulties that can arise when straying from the language of the legal test.

In respect of causation, ensure that you express your conclusions using the language of balance of probabilities. Terminology such as 'risk of', 'chance of' or 'possibility', is unhelpful. You need to be categoric when setting out your opinion. Avoiding vague language and sticking to the phrases in the legal tests themselves, will ensure there is no room for ambiguity and that time (and money) is not wasted clarifying your opinion. We want you to feel confident when faced with the other expert or indeed, if the case progresses to trial, under cross examination.

With regard to terminology, you should assume that the court knows nothing of your subject. Assume the same of your instructing solicitors. If appropriate, include a glossary and ensure that any abbreviations used are clearly explained.

Remember, if you have any doubts about your instructions you need to raise it with your instructing solicitors. It is preferable, rather than including any concerns you may have in the report itself, to discuss this via email or letter. This should enable you to report with clarity in the first instance and ensure there is a clear record of your discussion. It may be, for example, that you are missing paperwork or require evidence that has not been provided. You should raise this to enable you to report with clarity.

Consider the matter in the round

It will often be the case that, in the field of psychiatry, you will assess the injured party in person in the course of your report preparations. This will most likely be the most informative evidence you will have. However, your report needs to carefully consider all the factual evidence. This will include medical evidence and witness statements.

Context is everything. It may be that the comments and views of family members, whether in written evidence or in person, provide key information. Another critical thing to consider in your report is the timing of the incident. Your opinion needs to be based on what was known at that time and backed up by literature that was published at the time.

Conclusion

As the title of this chapter suggests, it is all about achieving balance. When preparing your report, think about it being placed in front of a judge. Think carefully about how you arrived at your conclusion, how you back that conclusion up and how you have considered other opinions. Remember expert immunity no longer exists (see chapter 16.)

This chapter should not be telling you anything fundamentally new or revolutionary, but rather act as guidance as to how best to prepare a balanced medico-legal report. Remember that your duty is to the court and that your audience - your instructing solicitor, the injured party, the other side and ultimately the court - is lay. Prepare your report accordingly. Take into account all the evidence available, consider all possible opinions and when arriving at your own conclusions, have the literature to support your view. Your opinion is critical.

Chapter 8 - Capacity reports - **Karen Shakespeare**

Lawyers are not famed for their willingness to admit they are not experts on everything, but if there is one area on which we are happy to obtain a second opinion, it is mental capacity.

When and why does a lawyer need a capacity report?

The most common reasons for seeking a capacity report are to check that our client has the ability to:

- make or alter a will (testamentary capacity)
- make a lasting power of attorney (**LPA**)
- deal with financial documents or enter into contracts
- engage in litigation
- consent to, or refuse, medical treatment
- enter into personal or sexual relationships

Each of these areas has a different legal test of capacity, a summary of which can be found in "Assessment of Mental Capacity: A Practical Guide for Doctors and Lawyers" (the 'AMC Guide'). This book is a joint publication by the British Medical Association and the Law Society, and is an essential reference for professionals dealing with medico-legal matters (see bibliography).

For lawyers, determination of mental capacity is somewhat complicated by the Mental Capacity Act 2005 (the MCA) which requires us to assume our clients are mentally capable, and to acknowledge their freedom to make unwise decisions. Add to this the fact that an individual's capacity may fluctuate over time (particularly through illness or medication), and you can see the problem (and of course no one wants to pay a solicitor to have several meetings in order to find a lucid window!). So how is a humble lawyer supposed to accurately assess capacity under these circumstances? It is no wonder that we seek a medical opinion on the legal tests.

Capacity reports – pre or post death?

A report on testamentary capacity can be required when someone is making a will, or when a will is being contested following the death of the testator (the person who made the will). Obviously it is much easier to assess testamentary capacity whilst the client is still alive, but this luxury is not always available, and unfortunately, many lawyers are reluctant to raise the subject of capacity with their clients.

Many may also be unaware at the time of drawing up the will that capacity could even be an issue.

Do lawyers recognise issues of capacity?

In short - not always. In a revealing and rather shocking three year study completed in 2012, solicitors and psychiatrists were shown videos of an elderly gentleman being interviewed. Two interview styles were recorded: 'good' and 'bad'. When shown the 'bad' interview, only 2% of solicitors (compared to 73% of psychiatrists) were able to recognise that the client had a lack of mental capacity. The study confirmed concerns held by litigation solicitor Robert Hunter (who had carried out the study along with consultant psychiatrist Dr Claire Royston), that solicitors often confuse social graces with mental ability. It also demonstrated the importance of asking the right questions and structuring a client interview in such a way that capacity issues might less easily be overlooked.

With aged testators, solicitors should be well aware of the risks involved in preparing a will. The 'Golden Rule' (which emerged from the 1975 contested will case of Kenward v Adams) is that where a solicitor is instructed to prepare a will for an elderly testator, a medical practitioner should witness the will. This rule has subsequently evolved into lawyers arranging for a medical practitioner to assess the testator's capacity and understanding, and to make a contemporaneous record of the examination and their findings.

GPs and capacity reports

For testamentary capacity reports, solicitors often instruct the testator's primary care physician, usually a GP. When working with a GP, a solicitor should provide:

- The relevant excerpt from the AMC Guide
- Information on the extent of the testator's estate
- A breakdown of what the testator's wishes are
- An explanation of whether these wishes differ from any earlier wills
- In relation to testamentary capacity, the AMC Guide sets out the test established in the 1870 case of Banks v Goodfellow, and requires that the GP answer the following:
- Does the testator understand that, by signing this document, they are making a will?
- Does the testator broadly know what they own?

- Has the testator considered the people they are including and excluding?

- In relation to this final question, does the testator have any condition or illness that could affect their decisions?

Solicitors are not always perfect however (which naturally shocks me!), and medical professionals should be prepared for the fact that they may be asked to write a testamentary capacity report without being given any guidance whatsoever. In these circumstances, they should refer to the AMC Guide themselves, and should ask the testator directly about their wishes and the reasoning behind them. Unfortunately, GPs are often unaccustomed to writing such reports, and unless the solicitor does ask clear and specific questions, this report is likely to be inadequate. I have seen GPs' (very short) letters confirming testamentary capacity deemed as worthless in subsequent court proceedings due to lack of detail or reference to specific issues.

Psychiatrists and capacity reports

Issues of brevity and lack of detail within a testamentary capacity report are not usually such a problem when a psychiatrist is involved, because they usually understand the legal tests they need to address. I recently dealt with a contested will case where the testator's GP and all of her family believed she had testamentary capacity, but a psychiatrist disagreed because he maintained that the testator did not understand the extent of her wealth. As the psychiatrist's report focused on the correct legal test of testamentary capacity it was accepted by the court - in preference to the evidence from her GP and her family.

When trying to establish testamentary capacity following the death of a testator, solicitors are therefore likely to instruct an expert psychiatrist because the report will need to undergo the scrutiny of the court.

What do lawyers need from psychiatrists?

For decisions under the Mental Capacity Act, solicitors need an expert opinion in relation to both the diagnostic test (section 4 MCA) and the functional test (section 5 MCA).

The diagnostic test determines that the client '*lacks capacity in relation to a matter if at the material time he is unable to make a decision for himself in relation to the matter because of an impairment of, or a disturbance in the functioning of, the mind or brain*'.

The functional test determines that the client *'is unable to make a decision for himself if he is unable (a) to understand the information relevant to the decision; (b) to retain that information; (c) to use or weigh that information as part of the process of making the decision; or (d) to communicate his decision (whether by talking, using sign language or any other means)'*.

It is interesting to note that in the Banks v Goodfellow test, the presence of a mental illness is only relevant if it affects the testator's decisions. Solicitors are therefore looking for psychiatrists to concentrate on this causal factor, rather than on the presence of the illness itself. I was involved in a case where a man with schizophrenia believed a group of strangers were plotting to murder him and he therefore wanted to make a will urgently. Although his motive for making the will was fuelled by his paranoid delusion, the terms of his will were not. He knew he was making a will, he knew the extent of his assets and he knew he wanted to benefit his close family members. He was therefore found to have testamentary capacity.

Conversely, I have seen cases where paranoid delusions have caused a testator to omit or remove from their will a relative who is deemed 'evil'. In this situation, the illness is extremely relevant to the issue of capacity.

How should a capacity report be structured?

There is currently no standard structure for a mental capacity report, and they differ from psychiatrist to psychiatrist. This, however, is the structure I find most convenient:

1.   Client's particulars

This section should contain a brief description of the person being assessed, including name, age, gender and marital status.

2.   Reason for the capacity report

This section should describe the decision or document, and the context of the legal proceedings. For example: 'The client wishes to make a new will to replace the will he made in 2005. He is changing his will because he no longer speaks to one of his daughters and wishes to exclude her from benefitting under his new will'.

The lawyer should have asked the client about any particular requirements they have. In the case of a lasting power of attorney, for instance, they should ascertain whether the client is making an LPA to deal only with finances, or in order to appoint someone who will also make decisions about their medical treatment. And, if the latter, whether they wish to include any particular instructions on the consent or refusal of treatment.

If a psychiatrist is asked to carry out such a capacity report and there are questions such as these which the lawyer does not appear to have addressed, he or she should ask for that information (rather than, as sometimes happens, simply writing a report which states that they do not have sufficient information to make the assessment!).

3.   Background information

This should include relevant details about the information gathered in relation to the report. For example:

- Information sources e.g. medical and social care records
- Notes from meetings with the client
- Notes from meetings with those who know the client (detailing relationship to the client)

- Client's academic, work, family and medical background
- Client's wishes, feelings, values, religious/cultural beliefs
- Summary of the relevant legal test of mental capacity
- Any other information provided by the solicitor

4.   Observations and diagnoses

In this section, the psychiatrist should note observations, examinations, conclusions and diagnoses. There should be a distinction made between observations or conclusions based on direct examination of the client and those based on information drawn from other sources.

5.   Opinion on mental capacity

This section should contain only the psychiatrist's opinion, not facts. It should include a statement as to whether the client has mental capacity to make the relevant decisions in relation to the legal situation outlined in section 2. There should also be clarification as to whether any mental health issues are relevant to those legal proceedings, or (as in the case of the paranoid client above) do not actually affect the client's ability in that specific area.

Where the client is found to lack capacity, there should be confirmation as to why and whether the client may recover that capacity at a later date. An example might be an elderly client whose ability to understand information has been temporarily disturbed by a chest infection.

Where the report is needed for court proceedings, a statement should be included which clarifies whether the client should be told about the court proceedings or whether this information may cause significant distress (and as such should not be revealed at this stage).

6.   Doctor's Particulars

And finally... this section should contain a brief summary of the acting psychiatrist's qualifications and experience, and, very importantly, the date of the report.

The future of capacity reports

As we have seen, psychiatrists have an important role to play in clarifying the mental ability of our clients. Early recognition of potential capacity issues, and the timely application of the correct legal tests, can minimise the heartache and expense involved in contested proceedings. Where capacity is unfortunately being determined after the fact, a psychiatrist's capacity report provides vital evidence on which to determine an equitable decision.

The simple fact that we are living longer means that the question of who can make decisions about an individual's medical treatment, for example, is of growing concern to our clients. This also remains a developing area of law, as the MCA continues to be tested in the courts, leaving judges to make decisions where the legislation has failed. The need for expert input from psychiatrists is therefore likely to increase as the population ages and the number of legal disputes continues to rise. GPs might be educated to fulfil this role, but psychiatrists will remain the most logical and able partner for solicitors in meeting their clients' needs.

Society's current desire (and expectation) of a quick, cheap, and easy solution to all their problems means that more and more people are choosing cut-price, or online, legal services where the question of capacity is simply not addressed. This is why wills, gifts and other financial transactions are increasingly disputed. The MCA has not made the situation any easier for solicitors either, as demonstrated by the number of cases involving LPAs and contested capacity. In this arena of confusion and risk, lawyers (and their clients) often need the help of a psychiatrist more than you may realise.

Chapter 9 - Criminal reports - **Julia Cox**

A criminal case is a case of two halves: the prosecution and the defence. The 'golden thread' running through all criminal cases is that the prosecution bring the case and have to prove the case against any defendant. The defence need not prove anything when it comes to the commission of an offence. All the defence are required to do is raise a doubt in the minds of the jury. However, even though the "golden thread" runs through all criminal cases, the defence are, in the majority of cases, the party who will initially require an expert psychiatric report. As a result, the majority of this chapter will focus on reports requested by the defence throughout the criminal justice process. A psychiatric report will not be required in every case where a defendant is charged, but when a report is necessary it will, broadly, fall into three categories: fitness to plead, criminal offences and sentence.

Fitness to plead

Prior to trial it will be necessary for the lawyers to consider whether a defendant has the required capacity to provide instructions, enter a plea and/or stand trial. Often there will be indicators from the outset that a particular defendant may be unfit to plead, but occasionally it will not become apparent until later in the proceedings. Where there are concerns that a defendant is unfit to plead a psychiatric report will be required to address that issue. The prosecution and defence are able to raise the issue as a preliminary point, but it is more likely that the defence will raise the issue as they will have more contact with the defendant enabling them to establish whether or not any concerns arise.

If an issue is raised about the defendant's fitness to plead or stand trial it will be necessary to prove to the satisfaction of the court that the defendant is unfit to plead. It is not a case of having to prove that a defendant is fit to plead; a judge is entitled to consider that a defendant is fit to plead without evidence from expert psychiatrist. It is essentially a situation where the defendant is presumed to be fit to plead until it is proven otherwise. In order to assess whether or not the defendant is fit to plead a court will need oral or written reports from at least two medical practitioners. Usually those medical practitioners will be psychiatrists. The reports will have to address the following points:

- Whether the defendant has sufficient intellect to instruct his solicitor and counsel

- Whether the defendant has sufficient intellect to plead to the indictment
- Whether the defendant has sufficient intellect to challenge jurors
- Whether the defendant has sufficient intellect to understand the evidence and
- Whether the defendant has sufficient intellect to give evidence

If the defence receive a report indicating that the defendant is unfit to plead then that report may be disclosed to the prosecution and the court. The defence are not required to disclose a report if it is not in the best interests of their client (the defendant), as the law currently stands. Therefore, if a report states that the defendant is fit to plead the criminal proceedings may continue without the contents of the report being disclosed. If the report indicates that the defendant is unfit to plead, the defence will advise the prosecution and the court, whilst obtaining the second report. This then gives the prosecution the option of obtaining a psychiatric report to either support or challenge the defence report.

Once the prosecution and the defence have their reports there will be a determination by the court. Where there is an agreement about the unfitness of the defendant to plead it will not be uncommon for the court to indicate that the defendant is unfit to plead without further argument. However, where there is disagreement there is likely to be a need for oral evidence to be given before the court. In practice, the issue of fitness to plead or stand trial will take place prior to the trial commencing to ensure that the trial is dealt with appropriately.

If a defendant is found to be unfit to plead the jury will have to consider whether or not the defendant did the act or made the omission with which he is charged. That is a different test to the test faced by defendants who are fit to plead and stand trial, as in those cases a jury will also have to consider the mental element of the offence. Therefore, it will often be the case that the issue of fitness to plead will be determined before trial. However, it can be left until the end of the prosecution case, if it is thought to be appropriate.

In some cases, the fitness or unfitness of a defendant may fluctuate. In these cases, it will be extremely difficult for the lawyers to be in a position to assess the defendant. If this is the case it is useful to include a section within the report highlighting the signs which would indicate that the defendant is becoming unfit to stand trial. Similarly, the defendant may be fit to stand trial but there may be limitations on their levels of concentration, for example. The last thing a lawyer requires at the end of a long day in court is for a defendant to say "I didn't understand anything that happened". If there are limitations, they should be addressed in the report. They may not lead to the conclusion that the defendant cannot understand the trial process, but if these matters are not addressed they will not always be recognised and could lead to the defendant being treated unfairly.

The role of a psychiatrist in circumstances where the defendant is fit to plead and stand trial, but has limitations, will always be important. The lawyers and the court will consider any recommendations that an expert can make to ensure that a defendant fully understands the trial process. If an intermediary is required then this is extremely important, but in the absence of a recommendation to that effect it will be extremely difficult for the lawyers to persuade a Court that the trial process should be adapted.

A report as to whether or not the defendant is fit to plead is not just a question of answering the criteria 'yes' or 'no'. The assessment process will inevitably involve a detailed analysis of the defendant's medical history and background as would be expected in every psychiatric report. The report, focusing on fitness to plead and fitness to stand trial, may conclude, on balance, that the defendant is fit enough to stand trial, but that they have limitations which mean that the trial process should be adapted. In these situations, the more detail present in the report with well-reasoned recommendations to assist a lawyer and ensure that the defendant has a fair trial, the better.

The offence

The criminal offences with which defendants are charged are broken down into two elements: the actus reus (the act) and the mens rea (the mental element). In order to be convicted of an offence both elements must have been proven beyond reasonable doubt. Whether a defendant is fit to plead or fit to stand trial or not, a jury will always have to consider whether the defendant committed the act. They only have to consider the mental element where a defendant is fit to plead.

Where a defendant has a fluctuating mental health condition and/or had other factors affecting cognitive function at the time of the offence, it may be appropriate to seek a psychiatric report to address whether, at the relevant time, the defendant could have formed the required intention to commit the offence. Reports of this nature can be relevant to all forms of offences; they are not limited to offences of murder. They can be appropriate for cases such as shoplifting, when the jury is required to consider whether or not the defendant was dishonest.

In these cases, the issue of whether the mental element of the offence has been established beyond reasonable doubt will be a question for the jury at a trial. However, a well-prepared and well-argued expert report dealing with this aspect of the case may, in some circumstances, be a bargaining tool on the part of the defendant leading to the prosecution reconsidering their case, and potentially accepting a guilty plea to an alternative lesser offence.

The ability to form the mental element of an offence may not, on the face of it, appear to be such an important issue when compared with the issue of whether or not a defendant is fit enough to stand trial. However, where a defendant is charged with a serious offence, which could lead to a lengthy term of imprisonment, and their defence is that they did not form the required intent, evidence from a psychiatrist casting a doubt on the defendant's ability to form that intent will be important.

Such evidence is likely to be challenged by the prosecution which may also obtain a report from another psychiatrist.

The court, when becoming aware of experts being involved in a case, will attempt to ensure that areas of agreement and disagreement are highlighted. However, it may be that oral evidence is likely to be required and an expert will have to face cross-examination as to how and why they have reached their conclusion. It will be cases such as these where the strength of an initial psychiatric report will be extremely important. A well-reasoned report with appropriate references will be more difficult to undermine and as such may carry more weight with a jury. The contents of a report and any oral evidence will be opinion evidence and the jury will have to conclude whether to accept or reject the opinion, but a well-argued report (or oral evidence) might carry greater weight.

Ultimately, the outcome may depend on the credibility of the defendant and his or her account of what was happening at the time of the alleged offence. If the jury concludes that the defendant's account is not credible there will be an obvious limitation to the weight of the evidence given by an expert as to whether the mental element of the offence can be established. In these cases, a conviction for a serious offence is unlikely to be a reflection of an expert's ability but rather to reflect the circumstances that the expert finds himself dealing with, whilst producing a report or giving evidence.

Sentence

The final part of the criminal process is, possibly, the most common area where psychiatric reports are obtained. The role of a psychiatrist in these circumstances is wide ranging. When considering any sentence the court is required to look at both punishment and rehabilitation. As such, it is often the rehabilitation aspect of the sentencing process that requires the input of a psychiatrist and the production of a report. The defence will often commission the psychiatric report, but the court can also direct that a report be obtained. The contents of the report should not differ on the basis of who has obtained it, as the overriding duty of any expert is to the court, not to the defence or the prosecution.

If the court directs that a psychiatric report be obtained, that report will be available to all parties, regardless of the contents and recommendations. The defence have no option but to allow the court to view it and consider it when passing sentence. Whereas, if the defence obtains the report themselves, with or without the court's knowledge, the legal requirements of disclosure mean that they are under no obligation to disclose the report to the court or to the prosecution if it is not in the best interests of their client.

The reports that are obtained in order to assist the court with passing sentence often ask specific questions of the psychiatrist with a view to establishing what type of sentence is appropriate. The evidence of psychiatrists will be required where consideration is being given to passing periods of detention or imposing remands under the Mental Health Act 1983 ('the Act'). In cases where a hospital order, under the Act, is being considered the defendant may have been remanded to hospital for a report to be prepared on his condition. In this case, the report will need to be completed by a psychiatrist, and should address the following points:

- Whether there is reason to suspect that the defendant is suffering from mental disorder
- Whether it is practical for a report to be prepared on bail

If the court were of the view the report can be prepared on bail there would be no need for a remand to hospital, but the report would still be required. Whether completed on bail or on remand the report would then be provided to the court so consideration could be given to the next steps.

In addition to a remand to obtain a report, the court also has the power to remand a defendant for treatment prior to sentence being passed. In these circumstances, reports will be required from two psychiatrists addressing two specific questions:

- Whether a defendant is suffering from a mental disorder which makes it appropriate for him or her to be detained in a hospital for medical treatment
- The appropriate treatment is available for him or her

The legal requirements indicate that one of the practitioners reporting must be one of the clinicians who will be taking overall responsibility for the defendant at the hospital. The report from this clinician will require confirmation of a place in hospital being available within seven days.

Following the remand for treatment, a further assessment is often undertaken by psychiatrists to consider whether or not a hospital order is an appropriate form of sentence. In these cases, two psychiatrists are required to prepare reports for the court addressing the following points:

- Whether the defendant is suffering from a mental disorder
- Whether there is reason to suppose that the mental disorder from which the defendant is suffering is such that it may be appropriate for a hospital order to be made in his or her case

Where those questions are answered to the effect that a hospital order may be appropriate, the court may make an interim hospital order before passing sentence. This will have the effect of allowing treatment to be undertaken for a maximum of 12 weeks in the first instance, with extensions available for 28 days at a time thereafter, up to a maximum of 12 months.

Following the interim hospital order, the court is then entitled to consider whether or not a final hospital is the appropriate means of disposal. In some cases, such an order will not be appropriate, as the treatment received under the interim hospital order may have been successful. However, in order to consider this, the court will require two reports from two psychiatrists, one of whom will be involved in the on-going treatment of the defendant. In considering the imposition of a final hospital order the court has to be satisfied on the evidence of two medical practitioners of the following:

- That the defendant is suffering from a mental disorder and that either-
  - The mental disorder from which the defendant is suffering is of a nature or degree which makes it appropriate for him to be detained in a hospital for medical treatment and appropriate medical treatment is available to him

    or
  - In the case of a defendant who is aged 16 years or over, is of a nature or degree which warrants his reception into guardianship
- The court is of the opinion having regard to all of the circumstances including the other methods of dealing with the defendant that the most suitable method of disposing of the case is by means of a hospital order.

In addition to considering whether a hospital order is the most appropriate method of disposal the court will also have to consider whether or not it is appropriate to attach a restriction order. These orders are reserved for the most serious offences, as the court has to consider whether a restriction order is necessary for the protection of the public from serious harm. If a restriction order is being considered two psychiatrists must prepare reports commenting on the appropriateness of the restriction order. At least one of those practitioners must attend court and give oral evidence about the imposition of a restriction order before the sentence is passed.

When reports are focusing directly on hospital orders, it is particularly important to ensure that all options are considered including whether or not a restriction order is required. The role of the psychiatrist is not limited to the imposition of orders under the Mental Health Act. Reports are often useful in assessing the reasons why the defendant has committed the offence. In addition, they can assist the court in determining whether or not a defendant is dangerous and needs a sentence, which protects the public from further offences.

If dangerousness is to be considered, for example as a result of the defendant being convicted of a number of serious violent offences, the defence may obtain a report from a psychiatrist with a view to establishing that the defendant is not dangerous. If a defendant is considered by the court to be a dangerous offender it has significant consequences. For example, the defendant may be sentenced to an extended sentence of imprisonment where they spend additional time in custody and will remain subject to an extended licence period. Alternatively, they may be sentenced to life imprisonment. In these circumstances, it is necessary to ensure that the court has all of the information available to them before a sentence is passed, especially if there is any suggestion that the defendant is not dangerous. Reports of this nature will invariably be asked to cover whether or not the defendant poses a significant risk of serious harm to members of the public by the commission of further offences. In addition, they will need to outline whether any courses or rehabilitation will assist the defendant in addressing the offending behaviour.

It is not in just the most serious cases where psychiatrists will be able to assist the court when it is determining sentence. Where a defendant appears before a court for an offence which is so completely out of character for that defendant, it may be that there are underlying concerns about the defendant's mental health. In these circumstances a report may be commissioned to assess whether there is an undiagnosed condition, which should be taken into account by the court. In addition, reports will occasionally be required to address whether a mental health treatment requirement will be an appropriate rehabilitative option as part of a community sentence or suspended sentence order. However, it should be borne in mind that the court is no longer required to have evidence from medical practitioners when passing a sentence which includes a community based mental health treatment requirement. As part of the sentencing process it is worth being aware that a psychiatric report will probably not be the only report being considered. A court will often also have a pre-sentence report prepared by a probation officer. If a pre-sentence report is available prior to an expert report being commissioned it may be useful to consider that report when finalising a recommendation for treatment and/or sentence.

Final thoughts

The scope of psychiatric reports in criminal cases is wide ranging. The purpose of this chapter has been to provide an overview as to how a psychiatric report can assist the court (and defendants) and to assist report writers in appreciating how their reports are used. However, the criminal law continues to develop and the use and availability of expert reports will evolve similarly. The important aspects of a psychiatric report will include an evaluation of the case papers, an analysis of the defendant's medical and social background and answers to the questions posed in a precise, clear, cogent and well-reasoned manner. If the purpose of the report is unclear it is incumbent upon the expert to clarify their instructions. Last, but by no means least, the expert must provide an unbiased and objective opinion so as to discharge their overriding duty to the court.

Chapter 10 - Psychiatry and neuropsychiatry reports in civil litigation - **Megan Goodyer**

Civil litigation covers a broad spectrum of legal proceedings. When psychiatrists and neuro-psychiatrists are required to prepare a report for legal proceedings, it will in most cases be for the civil courts for the purpose of personal injury litigation. Where experts are asked to submit a report to the Family Court or to an Employment Tribunal many aspects will be the same, though the emphasis of each report may be slightly different. These aspects are dealt with in later chapters of this book. For the purposes of this chapter the focus is on the preparation of a psychiatry or neuropsychiatry report as part of a personal injury claim. The majority of personal injury claims are for compensation of less than £20,000. In a typical case there is unlikely to be the involvement of a psychiatrist because the medical evidence is typically provided by an orthopaedic surgeon or a GP.

A psychiatrist is likely to become involved where a client has suffered a reaction to being involved in a serious accident from which they are struggling to recover. In the more traumatic cases, a psychiatrist or neuropsychiatrist may be asked to assess how somebody paralysed, or suffering a brain injury, as a result of the accident is adjusting to their condition. Even though the value of the claim may vary from £1,000 to £10 million the role of the expert remains the same. In basic terms the he or she is there to assist the court in confirming whether or not the individual has suffered the injury that is claimed, the prognosis of such an injury and the consequences of the injury in the long term. It is these consequences which the legal team will translate into financial losses following the accident.

Of all of the expert disciplines reporting most commonly in civil litigation, psychiatry can be one of the more partisan. An expert can, for example, be well known for having either a defendant or claimant bias. However, as the reader will know from having read other chapters, the duty of the expert is never to the paying party but is always first and foremost to the court.

Who is the report for?

In civil claims cases are dealt with in one of two ways: low value claims are dealt with in the fast-track, while higher value or more complex claims are dealt with in the multi-track. In low value fast-track cases it is more usual for the instruction of the psychiatrist to be included as a joint instruction.

Therefore, the psychiatrist will be instructed by both parties to assess the client and provide a report. In the multi-track process it is likely that the court will have provided permission for each party to obtain their own expert in the field. As psychiatry is often a contentious area single experts are more prevalent, with each party choosing to have their own expert. It is very unlikely that a neuropsychiatrist assessing a client following a brain injury would be requested to report in a fast-track case as the level of damages awarded would not merit their involvement.

It is important that the expert should know in which track the claim falls as this will have an impact on the recoverability of their fees. There are capped costs for preparing reports in the fast-track process. Whether the expert is being instructed either jointly or singly, their duty remains to the court. They are expected to provide the court with an independent, unbiased opinion which will assist in the assessment of the claim.

Is this case for me?

Perhaps the most important question that any expert should ask themselves when they receive a letter of instruction from their instructing solicitor is whether or not the client's case falls within their particular area of expertise. For example, a psychiatrist with only an adult psychiatry practice may not feel (or be) best placed to provide a diagnosis/prognosis for a young child following an accident (even if they hold a CCT [certificate of completion of training] in CAMHS [child and adolescent mental health services]). If the expert were to stray into an area outside of his or her expertise (which is based on experience and current practice as well as training) this will be picked up by the other party contesting the opinion and will be capitalised on during cross-examination, should the matter proceed to trial.

Psychiatrists or neuropsychiatrists may also find themselves conflicted as they may have treated one of the parties in the past. In such an instance, they should decline to accept instructions and inform the instructing solicitor immediately.

What does the report need to deal with?

From the lawyer's point of view, each report that is commissioned as part of the claim is likely to be done in order to estimate the value of the claim. What the legal team really wants to know is what the client's long-term prognosis is and how this this affects his or her everyday life. It is on the basis of this information that the claim can be calculated

Psychiatrists, or neuropsychiatrists, need to consider not only the present medical and psychiatric history of the client being assessed, but also their past history. In particular, are there any features in their past history which may be relevant to the problems from which they are currently suffering? The most common features in a client's pre-accident history which impact on their case are previous bouts of depression or anxiety or a record of alcohol or substance abuse. The likelihood is that if these features appear in the individual's medical history they will be well known to all of the parties and therefore should be acknowledged by the psychiatrist or neuropsychiatrist in their report, whether or not they are believed to have a bearing on the case. It is much better to raise these as issues and deal with them in full in report, responding to the questions: Do these pre-existing features relate to the individual's current difficulties and have they been exacerbated by the accident?

Next, the expert needs to deal with the causation of the injury. The expert has to address the question of whether the index accident or incident caused the injury which the client suffered. An individual is only successful in recovering damages if it can be shown that the injury sustained was caused by the accident. Often the issue of causation is clear cut and there is no doubt that the injury is a direct consequence of the accident. However, where there is relevant medical history which may indicate that the condition could have arisen in any event, causation may not be that straightforward. In this type of scenario the expert will be asked to consider what part of the injury is accident related and what is not. The expert may also be asked to look at whether the accident exacerbated a previous condition affecting the individual detrimentally.

The person's current condition and prognosis should be summarised for the court. If you believe that it is too early to provide a final prognosis, for example if treatment may improve the individual's condition, then it is worth stating this in your report and indicating to your instructing party when you feel that you will be in a better position to provide a final prognosis.

If treatment and on-going rehabilitation is required, this should be recommended together with the likely costs. If possible, it is also valuable to include in the report the likely outcome of any such treatment and the impact that any improvement may have on the client's presentation. When you are in a position to provide a view for the court on the final prognosis, the impact of the symptoms and difficulties should be considered, taking into account all areas of their life - health, work, family and leisure – and not only their ability to maintain employment or their family and domestic life. In the most serious of cases, your instructing team may ask you to consider the care and assistance which their client requires to help sustain the best quality of life possible.

The purpose of litigation and compensation is restorative. How do we offer the individual a life most closely approximating that which they had before their accident? This can only be done if all of the areas of their life that are affected by their condition are identified by the expert and steps to be taken are spelled out to enable recovery of the best possible quality of life.

What do I need?

In an ideal scenario you will be provided with a full letter of instruction with brief background details of the client explaining the psychiatric difficulties which have led to your instruction, together with all relevant medical and treating documentation. However, this ideal is rarely attained. If you feel that there are documents in existence which you have not been provided with, or documents which you would benefit from seeing or having prepared, you should let your instructing solicitor know. For example, you may benefit from a full witness statement from the client setting out the circumstances of the accident and their present difficulties.

Particularly in brain injury cases, you may wish to see witness statements from those close to the individual, for example statements from their case manager or their family. As you often have only a very short time within which to assess a person for the purpose of a medico-legal report, such documents can be invaluable in giving you a view into the individual's life on a day-to-day basis. It may be that the person themselves has little insight into their difficulties or is only partially able to give their history. Without the full and relevant documentation it is difficult to prepare an accurate report and failing to do so will only lead to adverse repercussions further down the line.

Lawyers are very good at demanding reports at the last minute and putting pressure on experts to prepare their reports quickly. It is worth setting out a reasonable timescale for the completion of your report as soon as you receive instructions so that both parties are clear and content when the report will be completed.

Top dos and don'ts

Keep it short

There is a tendency to repeat in your report a summary of all the documents that you have read highlighting the relevant sections. This is particularly true of those that deal with contentious issues and in which the weight of evidence for a particular opinion needs to be stressed. However, brevity will enable the reader to assimilate the argument quickly and avoid confusion about the conclusions that need to be drawn.

A report over 50 pages is too long and may not be read by a judge in full in the run-up to trial. In particularly complex cases it is useful to include your review of any documentation of particular relevance to the case in an appendix. It does not need to form the body of a report.

Don't delay

Wherever possible complete the report as soon after seeing the client as practicable. The longer the delay between seeing the client and preparing the report the more likely it is that the report will contain inaccuracies and will give rise to questions. If you are going to make treatment recommendations in the report, it is useful to have those recommendations made available to the client or their support network as soon as possible in order to avoid the client losing out on valuable treatment time.

Read the report

Although it is understandable that experts will copy and paste parts of their reports from other reports there is nothing that gets a solicitor's client offside more quickly than seeing a different person's name in their report or basic factual inaccuracies. Proof-reading does not take very long and will ensure that the individual does not immediately feel misunderstood.

Draft or final

If the report is only in draft form make sure that it is headed so. This will save you and your legal team being obliged to disclose a report that is not in its final form.

Changing your mind

If you change your mind about an opinion reached in your report let your legal team know straightaway and explain to them what has influenced the change. This is particularly important now that experts are no longer immune from suit (see chapter 16). If the change of opinion is likely to impact the claim negatively the solicitor, and their client in particular, will want to know what has caused the change of opinion. By the same token if you think that the conclusions you have reached in your report are not likely to be well received, it is worth calling your instructing solicitor in advance to warn them.

Keep it clear and concise

If a case proceeds to trial the judge is going to be asked to consider one party's report against the report prepared by the other party. The judge will have the responsibility of deciding whose evidence is more persuasive. He or she will want to have the arguments clearly presented and difficult issues explained. If the expert cannot communicate their view to the court effectively it may damage their solicitor's case. However complex and difficult the material is, the real skill of the expert lies in their ability to understand these complexities and explain their conclusions in the report and ultimately to the court.

Conclusion

The psychiatrist, or neuropsychiatrist, will provide the solicitor reading the report with their assessment of the impact of the accident or incident on all aspects of their client's life and also indicate appropriate treatment options. The bottom line is how much value this will add to the claim and whether or not the claim can be settled as soon as possible. The solicitors will want their expert evidence to be as persuasive as possible, well-reasoned, well-conceived and easy to understand, for the benefit of their client at the conclusion of the case.

Chapter 11 - Family reports - **Kirsty Richards**

Within family proceedings, there is often the need for expert opinion as the very nature of the proceedings will give rise to a number of issues relating to risk and safeguarding concerns for the child(ren) in the case. When it becomes apparent that an expert opinion is required to assist the parties and the court to understand the highlighted issues of case, the first question posed by lawyers is "Do you know a good expert?". The lawyers will usually then raise a series of names of experts they have used previously and discussions will take place as to the quality of the report, the timeliness of the report and the recommendations made, if any. For lawyers representing parents in public law proceedings (e.g. ss. 31-33 Children Act 1989 proceedings for care and supervision orders), a main consideration is the tone adopted in reports by the identified expert and whether they have been fair in their reporting.

The very fact that there are public law proceedings will suggest there is reason enough for a local authority to be concerned as to the welfare of the children of the family; sufficiently so that they have been able to satisfy the court that the threshold criteria has been met (s.31(2) Children Act 1989), and an assessment of the parent(s) in the case is now taking place to see whether there is any way the children can return to/remain with their parents and what level of support is required for that particular family. This is precisely why psychiatric reports are commissioned in family law proceedings as it allows the court and professionals to have a good understanding as to why that particular parent has behaved/parented in the manner in which they presented in the lead up to the issue of formal court proceedings. The very essence of the Children Act 1989 reminds professionals involved in public child law cases that removal of children from their parents must be the order of last resort, and should not be taken lightly.

With that said, the courts will often approve the care plans of local authorities that provide for children to be placed in foster care pending assessment of the parents; preferring to err on the side of caution with regard to the perceived risks identified by the local authority which brought the case into the court arena. For most parents, that will often mean that they are indeed separated from their children at the very early stages of proceedings and are suddenly immersed into a world of intense assessments by local authorities, independent social workers and psychiatrists. For many of those parents, the outset of proceedings is extremely frightening and it can be a shock for many of those to be told that they need to now meet with a psychiatrist in order for the parties to have an understanding as to the management of the safeguarding risks identified in the case.

Parents will often struggle with the suggestion of engaging with a psychiatric assessment. They express anxiety as to what the assessment process will involve and the overriding concern seems to be the fear that the expert will identify problems which will mean the child(ren) of the family may be unable to return home. For many, this is their first exposure to any formal psychiatric assessment and they will often ask lawyers to find a "nice, understanding expert" who will not immediately judge them on the case papers and render the assessment process hopeless in terms of their aim to get the court to sanction the return of the children to their care.

This is when lawyers will often ask each other, having agreed the identity of the psychiatric expert on the basis of their circulated CV, whether that expert will provide mum or dad with a fair report, or whether such a report is likely to provide the court with evidence which is ultimately unhelpful in assessing whether it is safe for the children to return home. In saying that an expert provides a fair report, lawyers will mean that the identified expert has considered all the issues in the case and has explored them with the parent(s) in the course of the assessment process. That assessment will have allowed the parent to think about the issues raised by professionals in depth, allowing a full and frank discussion between the parent and the expert.

The expert who produces a fair report will have not prejudged the parent(s) on the case papers and will have instead presented the parent(s) with an opportunity to engage in a full and frank discussion about everything that has occurred in their lives and in particular, in the months/years prior to the issue of proceedings. Fair reports will be written in a tone which demonstrates that the expert used their best endeavours to encourage the parent(s) to provide full answers and entered into a detailed discussion about the issues at hand. If a parent has struggled to engage with the assessment process, it is helpful for lawyers to see reference in the report to the attempts made to get the parent(s) to engage and therefore the expert should provide as much information as possible in their reports to enable the lawyers to understand this process.

Most lawyers who represent parents in public law proceedings will have already advised their clients as to the nature of the psychiatric assessment and what is expected of them in order to allow the expert the opportunity to provide a full and fair report to the court. It is encouraging to receive feedback from parents that the expert they have seen has been welcoming and took the time to explain his or her role and the need for an honest discussion if there is to be any hope of producing a fair report. Clearly, failure to provide full answers to questions posed will make the expert's job more difficult in terms of being able make a diagnosis or any recommendations. When experts have explained this, parents will often report back to their lawyer that they then realised the importance of engaging fully in the process.

Where parents have had the opportunity to understand the nature of their psychiatric assessment, the reports will generally be accepted as fair and can then be fed into the other assessments taking place; providing the family court with a good base of written evidence upon which to make its decision as to the long term plans for the child(ren) in the case.

It is really helpful if experts can provide examples of the parent's responses to the questions posed as it can be extremely insightful to read the actual words offered by the parents. This aids a sound understanding as to how the expert has then gone on to reach the conclusion they have reached, be it positive or negative, in terms of possible reunification for the family. Particularly when the expert has identified that the parent has indeed got a psychiatric condition, it is essential for the parties to be able to gain an understanding as to whether there is any possibility for that parent to learn the appropriate skills necessary to ensure they are able to offer consistently good enough parenting to the child(ren).

Often the questions posed within the agreed letter of instruction will ask the expert to consider what treatment, if any, could be offered to the parent and what timescales are involved. It is also essential to know about the precise details of any proposed ongoing treatment and whether it is so intense that the parent would be best placed to engage with that treatment with the children remaining in alternative placements; or whether it is possible for the children to be returned home whilst the parent(s) engage with treatment.

The considerations to be considered here are those surrounding the intensity of any proposed treatment, the length of time the parent(s) will need to engage with it and whether that treatment will lessen in intensity after a period of time etc.

As the ethos of the Children Act 1989 asks professionals to consider what support can be put in place to allow children to remain within their birth family, it is vital for all writers of expert family reports commissioned in the case to have that understanding at the forefront of their minds so that professionals and experts are all coming at the case from the same angle.

It can be extremely unhelpful to receive a psychiatric report which makes a diagnosis but provides little detail as to whether a robust support/therapy package could be put in place over a period of time which may then provide for reunification of the family. In circumstances where the expert considers the parent would be unable to meet the needs of the child(ren), it is especially helpful to have the maximum amount of information as to why that is the case as it will undoubtedly have serious implications for the child(ren) in the case.

The psychiatric expert for the parent(s) should ask the lawyers instructing them if there is a child and adolescent psychiatric expert appointed in the case and/or whether there is any evidence as to the specific needs of the children, as that evidence will be useful in ascertaining the level of parenting required. Similarly, there will usually be some evidence available as to the current parenting ability being demonstrated by the parent as they tend to be referred for a parenting assessment early on in proceedings. It is reassuring to read reports which confirm that the expert has read all other assessments and has considered these alongside their own assessment notes.

The adult psychiatric expert should avoid going outside their area of expertise and commenting on parenting ability and risk to the child(ren) – except from within their (limited) area of expertise. It is much safer to instead provide their own psychiatric analysis and state the other evidence considered, quoting passages. It is also far better for experts to state in reports that a particular question is outside their area of expertise than to risk offering opinions about risk and parenting which could have serious implications for the family at the heart of the assessment process.

Aside from the need for family reports to be fair, there is a pressing need for the report to be produced in a timely fashion, often due to the parties needing to have a clear understanding as to a parent's emotional wellbeing for the purposes of arranging contact (as well as the long term placement needs of the child(ren).

Lawyers will always ask how long the report will take and will often be persuaded to instruct the expert most able to report quickly (and within the agreed Legal Aid Agency rates). The parent(s) involved in the case will usually instruct lawyers to proceed with the expert most able to get the report finalised as soon as possible. For many parents, the anxieties surrounding the psychiatric assessment will lead them towards wanting to get it over and done with as quickly as possible, including the receipt of the actual report (despite them being extremely anxious about receiving the report as it will usually dictate the direction of the rest of the case).

The use of family reports in any Children Act proceedings is often vital to the decision-making process for the parties involved in reaching a decision as to the long term care plans for the child(ren) of the case. A good report is most definitely a fair report and fair reports can be achieved if the expert is conscious of the overriding objective as set out in s.1 of the Children Act 1989:

When a court determines any question with respect to -
(a) the upbringing of a child; or
(b) the administration of a child's property or the application of any income arising from it,

the child's welfare shall be the court's paramount consideration.

Chapter 12 - Immigration reports - **Leonie Hirst**

Introduction

Expert reports are playing an increasingly prominent role in immigration cases, and a cogent and comprehensive psychiatric report can make the difference between a successful case and an unsuccessful one. This chapter outlines the different contexts in which a psychiatric report may be requested in an immigration case, highlights some relevant legal principles and gives some suggestions as to what immigration lawyers and courts are looking for from a psychiatric expert.

Types of immigration case

Psychiatric reports may be required in immigration cases in a wide variety of contexts, and what is needed in a report will often depend on the type of case which is being brought. A brief disclaimer: the following is not intended to be a comprehensive guide to what is an increasingly complex area of law, but is simply intended to provide a brief summary of the legal context in which a psychiatric report may be required, to help report writers understand the context in which the report will be used.

Human rights claims

Claims in which psychiatric input is required will broadly fall into one of three categories. The first category is a human rights claim. These are cases in which the individual claims that his or her rights under the European Convention on Human Rights ('ECHR') are or will be breached because of a refusal to allow him/her to enter the UK, to grant leave to remain in the UK, or (more commonly) a decision that he/she should be deported or removed from the UK.

Psychiatric reports are most likely to be required in cases raising claims under Articles 2 (the right to life), 3 (the prohibition on torture or inhuman or degrading treatment) or 8 (the right to respect for one's family and private life). Article 2 ECHR guarantees the right to life. Article 2 imposes not simply a negative obligation on states to refrain from taking life, but a positive obligation to protect life. This means that state authorities owe a duty of care to individuals where there is a potential risk of death arising from suicide or self-harm; this is particularly relevant in the context of immigration detention, which is dealt with in more detail below. Article 2 may also be engaged by the state's denial of health care to immigrants/asylum seekers or by the failure to provide sufficient resources for necessary care.

Article 3 provides protection from torture or inhuman or degrading treatment or punishment. In immigration cases raising mental health issues, Article 3 is most often engaged by medical treatment (or lack of treatment), or by the lack of treatment or facilities available in the country of origin. For example, an asylum seeker with mental illness may claim that return to his country of origin would breach his Article 3 rights because there is no treatment or medication available there and his condition would therefore deteriorate sharply. There is a relatively high threshold for Article 3 to be engaged; what is required is treatment which reaches 'a minimum level of severity' and involves intense suffering. Recently, claimants in several cases have successfully challenged their detention under immigration powers on the basis that detention, and the lack of treatment or medication, has resulted in suffering which breached Article 3.

Article 8 protects an individual's right to respect for his private and family life. Unlike Articles 2 and 3, Article 8 is a 'qualified' right; that is, interference with Article 8 rights may be justified if it is proportionate and pursuing a legitimate aim. As part of his private life, an individual has the right to respect for his 'physical and moral integrity', which encompasses mental health. An Article 8 claim may therefore raise mental health issues which do not meet the high threshold for a claim under Article 3.

Asylum claims

The second category of immigration case in which a psychiatric report may be requested is asylum claims, in which an applicant seeks protection under the Refugee Convention. To succeed in an asylum claim, an applicant must demonstrate that he or she has a well-founded fear of persecution for reasons of race, religion, nationality, membership of a particular social group, or political opinion in his or her country of origin, and that he or she cannot obtain protection from the authorities. A successful asylum claim results in the applicant being recognised as a refugee. The Refugee Convention, and the Qualification Directive, prohibit the return of a refugee to the country in which he/she fears persecution, and the Secretary of State's current practice is to grant leave to remain in the UK for an initial period of five years which may be extended.

In addition to refugee status, the Qualification Directive requires EU (European Union) member states to provide subsidiary protection to people who do not qualify as refugees but who face a real risk of serious harm and cannot obtain protection in their home country; in the UK this is implemented as 'humanitarian protection'. A successful claim for humanitarian protection results in the grant of leave to remain, usually for a period of three years.

Psychiatric reports may be required in an asylum claim to help corroborate the applicant's account. For example, where an individual claims to be suffering from post-traumatic stress disorder as a result of traumatic experiences in his or her country of origin, a psychiatric report may be required to confirm the diagnosis and also to comment on the likelihood that the symptoms observed are caused by the reported trauma.

Psychiatric reports may also be required in an asylum claim where an expert opinion is required on the availability of treatment in the country of origin or the likely impact on mental health of returning the asylum claimant to their country of origin.

Immigration detention

The third category of immigration case in which psychiatric reports are increasingly important is claims arising from immigration detention. The Secretary of State has broad powers, under the Immigration Act 1971, the Nationality, Immigration and Asylum Act 2002 and the UK Borders Act 2007, to detain individuals in a range of different situations. Individuals can be detained on entry to the UK pending examination by an immigration officer and a decision on whether to allow them to enter. In some cases, individuals can be detained whilst their asylum claim is considered within the so-called 'Fast Track' procedure. Individuals can also be detained pending deportation or administrative removal; the latter is a broad category which includes those illegal entrants and those who have overstayed their leave.

In the UK, around 28,000 people enter and leave immigration detention each year. There is no limit to how long an individual may be detained under immigration powers; whilst the majority of individuals are detained only for relatively short periods (up to a month), some may be detained for many months or even years. Perhaps unsurprisingly, there is significant evidence from both the UK and elsewhere (e.g. Steel & Silove, The mental health implications of detaining asylum seekers. Medical Journal of Australia, 175, 596 -599, Sultan & O'Sullivan, 2001 Psychological disturbances in asylum seekers held in long term detention: a participant-observer account. Medical Journal of Australia, 175, 593 -596. Keller, A. S., Rosenfeld, B., Trinh-Shevrin, C., et al (2003) Mental health of detained asylum seekers. Lancet, 362, 1721 - 1723, Robjant et al, 2009, 'Psychological Distress amongst Immigration Detainees: A cross sectional questionnaire study'. British Journal of Psychology 48:275-86) that detention, particularly prolonged detention, has a significant impact on the mental health of immigration detainees. Despite the evidence, and despite the high incidence of mental illness amongst detainees, people continue to be detained for long periods.

Psychiatric input/reports are required in immigration detention cases in three contexts:

- A report may be required for a transfer of an immigration detainee to hospital under s.48 Mental Health Act 1983.

- A report may be needed as to whether the detainee's mental health renders him or her unfit for detention or unfit for removal from the UK. Under Rule 35 of the Detention Centre Rules, the medical practitioner in a detention centre is obliged to report to the manager of the centre on any detainee who is at risk of suicide, or whose health is likely to be injuriously affected, by detention. A psychiatric report from an independent expert may be necessary to alert the medical practitioner in the detention centre to a detainee's deteriorating mental health, in order to trigger a Rule 35 report, or to support the view of the medical practitioner that detention is no longer appropriate.

- A psychiatric report is commonly required when an individual wishes to challenge the lawfulness of his or her detention. This is because, under the so-called 'Hardial Singh principles', the Secretary of State and the courts are required to consider the impact of detention on the individual detainee when assessing whether it is reasonable and lawful to continue to detain that individual.

In the tribunal: the role of the psychiatric expert and psychiatric evidence

As outlined above, psychiatric reports may be required in a wide variety of contexts and in cases raising a wide variety of issues. They may also be required at different stages of a case, and it can be helpful if experts understand what stage a case is at when they provide an expert report.

The first stage is an application or claim. In some cases this can be made on paper, by written submissions to the Secretary of State via the Home Office; in asylum cases, however, the Secretary of State's policy is to require a claim to be made in person. If a claim is accepted, then the Secretary of State will decide on the relevant grant of leave and the case is unlikely to reach court. However, if a claim is rejected, and the individual has a right of appeal, the case will come before the First Tier Tribunal.

If the First Tier Tribunal dismisses the appeal, the appellant can seek permission to appeal from the Upper Tribunal on the basis that the First Tier Tribunal has made an error of law. If the Upper Tribunal grants permission to appeal, it will review the decision of the First Tier Tribunal and decide whether there has been a material error of law; if so, it will decide whether it can remake the decision on the evidence before it, or whether a fresh hearing is required. A further appeal lies to the Court of Appeal (or the Court of Session in Scotland).

It is unusual for psychiatric experts to be required to give oral evidence in the First Tier or Upper Tribunals, and so usually the Tribunal will only have the benefit of the expert's written report. Whilst it is not uncommon for the Secretary of State to disagree with expert psychiatric evidence, it is highly unusual for the Secretary of State to obtain or serve psychiatric evidence. This means that the role of the psychiatric expert report in immigration proceedings is different to that of other civil proceedings, such as a personal injury claim in the county court. There is little opportunity for an expert to be cross-examined or face written questions from the other side; it will often be unclear whether and on what basis his opinion is disputed until the hearing itself. It is therefore even more important in Tribunal proceedings that a psychiatric expert report is clear, unambiguous and sufficiently reasoned.

There have been a number of cases which define how the Tribunal should approach evidence from psychiatric experts. It is important to remember that the Tribunal is not obliged to accept expert evidence; fact-finding remains the province of the adjudicator even where psychiatric evidence is concerned. However, the tribunal must give due weight to the opinion of a psychiatric expert; it cannot, for example, simply dismiss a psychiatric opinion as 'speculation' without good reasons and evidence for doing so. Similarly, if the tribunal chooses to reject the evidence of a psychiatric expert, it must give a cogent explanation why it does so, particularly (as in most cases) where there is no opposing psychiatric evidence.

Where psychiatric evidence is available, the tribunal should consider that evidence before it reaches any conclusion on an appellant's credibility; it should not conclude that an appellant is unreliable or untruthful and then assess medical or psychiatric evidence in light of that conclusion. In *Y and Z (Sri Lanka) v Secretary of State* [2009] EWCA Civ 362, Lord Justice Sedley emphasised the importance of psychiatric experts' professional expertise in assessing and diagnosing patients; it is not open to the tribunal judge, who will not normally have psychiatric expertise, to form a view for himself that an appellant is feigning or exaggerating symptoms in contradiction to the view of psychiatric experts.

The contents of the report

In common with other types of case, the psychiatric expert's duty in an immigration case is to the court. What is required was summarised in the 'Ikarian Reefer case' and the principles are well-known. Overall, expert evidence presented to the court should be, and should be seen to be, the independent product of the expert, who should provide assistance to the court by way of his or her objective unbiased opinion on matters within his or her expertise. This cannot be emphasised enough. In an immigration context, psychiatric experts are usually instructed by the claimant or appellant; however, the expert should resist any temptation to advocate on behalf of the claimant or appellant, as any perception by the tribunal of partiality on the part of the expert undermines the weight which is given to his or her evidence.

Similarly, it is important that the psychiatric expert does not seek to 'usurp' the role of the judge by giving an opinion on matters which are properly the jurisdiction of the court. A psychiatric expert may properly, for example, give an opinion about whether an individual is feigning or exaggerating psychiatric symptoms; he or she cannot properly give an opinion about the credibility of the individual's account of past persecution, which is for the court to assess.

The psychiatric expert should state facts or assumptions upon which his or her opinion is based, and should also consider material facts which could detract from his or her concluded opinion. An expert should make it clear when a particular question or issue falls outside his or her area of expertise, and if insufficient data is available to form a proper opinion he/she should state that the opinion given is provisional. Any qualifications to the expert's opinion should be clearly stated in the report.

What makes a good report?

A good psychiatric report, in the immigration context, is one which is clear, precise, detailed and carefully reasoned. In many cases, the form and structure of the report are nearly as important as the content of the psychiatric opinion, and the difference between a successful report and an unsuccessful one is often no more than a few paragraphs of additional detail.

It is important for psychiatric experts to remember that immigration tribunals are 'lay' tribunals. It is not uncommon, particularly in asylum cases, for appellants to exhibit symptoms of depression or posttraumatic stress disorder, and some tribunal judges may consider themselves relatively familiar with these conditions. However, diagnosis of psychiatric conditions is properly the province of the psychiatric expert; there is an obvious distinction between the clinical opinion of an experienced and qualified expert, based on a proper assessment of the individual in a clinical context, and the judge's lay opinion based on his or her visual assessment of the individual giving oral evidence in court. Where a report contains a clinical diagnosis or refers to recognised psychiatric conditions, it is often helpful to provide a brief (and properly referenced) explanation. This is particularly true where the lay understanding of a condition may not be adequate or sufficiently nuanced; for example, the difference between a moderate depressive episode and a severe depressive episode is not immediately clear to the lay person and should be explained by reference to diagnostic criteria.

The psychiatric report should make clear the basis of any diagnosis or opinion. Where an individual has been assessed, the report should state when, where and for how long the individual was seen. It is relatively common for an expert's opinion to be rejected by the Tribunal on the basis that he or she has seen the individual only on one or two occasions for a short time. If there is no ongoing clinical relationship with the individual, it is therefore helpful if the expert can confirm that a full assessment was possible in the time available. Where there are issues on which it was not possible to reach a conclusion in the time available, the expert report should, of course, make this clear.

Where diagnostic tools have been used, the report should state clearly what those are; where a particular tool is not validated for use with that particular client (for example, because of language/interpretation issues or learning difficulties) the expert should consider whether it is necessary to use it, and set out carefully any qualifications in his or her opinion. Where an assessment is conducted via an interpreter, it is very important that the psychiatric expert considers the impact of the interpreter's presence on the individual's responses and the rhythm of the assessment.

It is common for a psychiatric expert to be provided with (non-medical) documents relating to the case, to give the expert an idea of the context and background of the claim. These might include, for example, the individual's witness statement setting out the basis for his asylum or human rights claim, or the Secretary of State's letter refusing his claim. The expert should list all documents considered at the beginning of the report. It is very common for expert opinions to be rejected by the Tribunal on the basis that they have adopted the appellant's account uncritically. It is therefore helpful if an expert can make it clear that whilst he has read relevant documents, he is aware that parts of the appellant's account are disputed by the Secretary of State and that he has not based his psychiatric assessment on the assumption that the appellant's account is true. It is preferable for a psychiatric report to avoid referring to the facts of the appellant's claim altogether if possible, since any apparent inconsistency between the facts set out in the appellant's statements and the facts as recounted by the psychiatric expert can and will be relied on by the Secretary of State in court to undermine the appellant's case.

It is also important that a psychiatric report sets out clearly the expert's expertise, specialisation and qualifications which enable him or her to give an expert opinion on the matters in his or her report. For example, where an asylum applicant claims to be experiencing symptoms of posttraumatic stress disorder as a result of past torture, the expert should state clearly his or her expertise and past experience in assessing mental illness arising from torture. It is very important that experts consider, prior to accepting instructions, whether, in fact, they have the requisite expertise or experience to assess the individual concerned. A psychiatrist with experience of assessing adult refugees, for example, may not be best placed to give a proper opinion on a child or adolescent claimant. The expert in these circumstances should make the limits of his or her expertise clear to the instructing solicitor, to minimise the chances that the psychiatric report is subsequently rejected by the tribunal. Where the evidence of the psychiatric expert has been accepted by a tribunal in previously reported cases, it is helpful for those to be cited and referred to in the qualifications section of the report.

The report should set out the questions on which the expert has been asked to advise and give a clear and precise opinion. Ideally, the report should use numbered paragraphs or sections so that it can be referred to more easily in court, and should be structured so that it is easy for the tribunal to find the expert's conclusions and reasoning. Again, it is important for the expert to understand that he or she is unlikely to be giving oral evidence in court; it is therefore vital that the report is sufficiently clear and detailed that it is unambiguous and easily understood by a lay tribunal.

Particular issues may arise in some cases relating to the causation of psychiatric illness; for example, where an appellant suffers posttraumatic stress disorder as a result of persecution in his country of origin, or where immigration detention exacerbates a pre-existing psychiatric condition. In some cases it may be possible for the psychiatrist to comment on whether the illness or condition has been caused by the events described, but it is more helpful to avoid referring directly to causation, which is properly the province of the tribunal as fact-finder. Psychiatric evidence should focus, not on causation, but on whether symptoms or a condition are consistent with the appellant's account.

Where there is a clear diagnosis of a post-traumatic condition, for example, the psychiatric expert should attempt to find out whether the appellant has been exposed to other traumatic events which might have caused or precipitated the condition; the report can then state that there is a diagnosis which is highly consistent with a past traumatic experience of the type described and that the appellant does not report any other traumatic events which might explain the diagnosed symptoms. Again, all aspects of the psychiatric opinion need to be clear, detailed and carefully reasoned.

Obviously, where other studies or literature are referenced to support an opinion, these should be properly and fully cited; where these are relied on in detail, it is very helpful, and adds weight to the psychiatric report, if a copy of the relevant passage or article is annexed to the report. It cannot be emphasised enough that the report must be clear, concise and adequately reasoned. A report which simply gives a diagnosis, without explanation or further consideration, is unhelpful to the Tribunal and unlikely to assist either party. It is important that the expert sets out clearly the basis for his or her opinion, gives reasons for his conclusions and considers how the evidence may be received by the tribunal.

Common pitfalls

As outlined above, the tribunal is not bound to accept the evidence of a psychiatric expert. However, where psychiatric reports are rejected, it is usually because the expert has made one of the following mistakes. Avoid these common pitfalls and it is more likely that your expert report will assist the Tribunal and the appellant:

Matters outside expertise

Do not comment on matters which are outside your expertise or instructions. If, during the preparation of the report, it becomes apparent that you may be able to comment on an area which is not within your initial instructions, contact the instructing solicitor and check with him/her whether the additional matter should be included in the report. However, it is vital that experts resist the temptation to comment on matters of which they have no experience or expertise. If your instructions ask you to comment on a matter which is not within your expertise, explain in the report that you are unable to comment and explain why.

Reports based on factual accounts

Reports are commonly rejected for appearing to be based on the appellant's factual account of past experiences. It is the tribunal's job to assess the appellant's factual account, not the psychiatric expert. Ideally your report should be confined to matters which you can assess for yourself within your clinical expertise and experience. Keep references to the appellant's past experiences to a minimum and only refer to them when necessary to support a clinical diagnosis. Where necessary, state clearly in the report that you have understood that the appellant's account is disputed by the Secretary of State.

Reports based on subjective symptoms

Similarly, avoid any suggestion that your clinical diagnosis is based entirely on self-reporting of symptoms by the appellant. Whilst in most cases a diagnosis will of necessity depend on reported symptoms, it is important to note symptoms which are evident during examination and record whether these are consistent with the appellant's description. A failure to make it clear that your opinion is based on observation and assessment, rather than a recorded history, is likely to lead to the rejection of your report.

Use of 'technical terms'

Do not assume that the tribunal will necessarily understand what you mean when you refer to particular symptoms or use technical language. The tribunal may not be familiar with the particular technical meaning of words such as 'arousal' or 'hypervigilance'. A short and clear explanation will avoid misunderstanding and provide greater assistance to the tribunal.

Longwinded and poorly-structured reports

Do not present the tribunal with a 'stream of consciousness' report which is discursive and difficult to read or understand. Always structure the report clearly and set out your conclusions in a separate summary at the end of the report.

Imprecise and emotional language

Do not 'waffle' or exaggerate, and avoid overly emotive language. The tribunal is much more likely to accept expert evidence which is couched in objective and dispassionate terms. A report which suggests that the expert has gone beyond his or her objective role and is advocating on behalf of the appellant is likely to be rejected.

The key thing to remember is to keep the report clear and sufficiently reasoned. Always make the basis for your opinion clear and explain your reasoning fully. Above all, bear in mind that the role of the psychiatric expert is to provide an objective and unbiased opinion and to assist the court, rather than the appellant.

Chapter 13 - Employment reports - **Andrew Berk**

Background to employment tribunals

Employment tribunals are the main forum in which
employment disputes between (ex-)employees ('claimants) and
(ex-)employers ('respondents') are resolved. They were set up
in the 1960s and their purpose was to, *"... provide an easily
accessible, speedy, informal and inexpensive procedure for the settlement of
employment disputes. "* (Donovan Commission).

Employment tribunals have jurisdiction to hear in excess of 70
types of claims, the main ones being: unfair dismissal;
redundancy; all forms of discrimination including: sex, race,
disability and age, unlawful deductions from wages, working
time matters and family friendly rights. The employment
tribunals do not have jurisdiction to hear personal injury
claims although certain types of discrimination claims such as
sex, race and disability discrimination, may include an award
to reflect personal injury, often to compensate for psychiatric
harm.

There has been a very substantial increase in the number of
employment tribunal claims in recent years. In 1989, there

were less than 40,000 whereas the latest government statistics show that in 2011/2012, there were 186,300 claims having gone down slightly from 236,100 claims in 2009/2010. The government plans to introduce fees shortly in the employment tribunals in an attempt to reduce the burden of running the Employment Tribunal Service on the taxpayer and to deter unmeritorious and vexatious claims.

Claims in the employment tribunals have never been subject to any tracks unlike claims in the civil courts which are allocated to the various tracks depending on their financial value. Compensation for unfair dismissal claims is capped at £87,700 and there is currently a Government proposal to cap it further at 12 months' pay or £74,200.

On the other hand, there is no limit on the amount of compensation that can be awarded in discrimination claims by virtue of European law. Government statistics for 2011/2012 show that the average awards of compensation were as follows: unfair dismissal = £9,133; sex discrimination = £9,940; race discrimination = £102,259; and disability discrimination = £22,183.

Disability discrimination and the rise of medical experts in the employment tribunals

Traditionally, medical experts rarely appeared in employment tribunals cases. One might have seen them occasionally in claims for sexual and racial harassment when medical evidence would have been required to analyse the extent of any psychological injury and harm allegedly caused to the claimant by the respondent and any long-term effects and whether the claimant could continue in their role. However, there suddenly became a much greater need for medical evidence with the advent of the Disability Discrimination Act 1995.

This act was the first domestic act on the issue of disability discrimination, prior to which it was legal to discriminate and exclude on the basis of disability even including in employment. It was introduced to bring this country into line with European legislation. Unsurprisingly, the Disability Discrimination Act 1995 caused a lot of controversy particularly in view of the often significant costs for employers in having to modify buildings and vehicles to accommodate disabled employees as the effect of the legislation was to significantly increase the access of many people to the labour market.

The Disability Discrimination Act 1995 described a disabled person as someone with, 'a physical or mental impairment which has a substantial and long-term adverse effect on his ability to carry out normal day-to-day activities', which has lasted, or can be expected to last, for more than 12 months. Conditions that impair an individual's abilities in this way include: those that hamper mobility, manual dexterity, physical co-ordination, continence, the ability to lift, carry or move everyday objects, speech, hearing or eyesight, memory or ability to concentrate, learn or understand and understanding of the risk of physical danger. Examples of disabilities include: heart disease, motor neurone disease, HIV and AIDS, asthma, dyslexia, depression, obsessive compulsive disorder, autism, myalgic encephalomyelitis (ME)/chronic fatigue syndrome (CFS), fibromyalgia, depression, epilepsy schizophrenia and eating disorders.

The various anti-discrimination laws in this country have now been consolidated into the Equality Act 2010 as amended. The types of discrimination that are prohibited include:

- Direct discrimination - where an employer treats an employee less favourably because of a protected characteristic e.g. sex, race, disability etc. An example would be an employer denying a disabled employee a promotion because of that employee's disability

- Indirect discrimination - where an employer applies a provision, criterion or practice which is discriminatory in relation to the employee's protected characteristic and which the employer cannot show to be a proportionate means of achieving a legitimate aim. An example would be an employer's practice of not allowing any female employees to do overtime

In addition, disability discrimination also allows a claimant to make a claim for discrimination arising from disability. This is where an employer treats an employee unfavourably because of something arising in consequence of the employee's disability and the employer cannot show that the treatment is a proportionate means of achieving a legitimate aim. An example would be an employee refusing a visually-impaired employee to have a guide dog because the employer is concerned that there is insufficient space in the office for the dog.

Further, an employer has a duty to make reasonable adjustments for a disabled employee. An example would be an employer allowing a disabled employee to work with specially-adapted work equipment.

In addition, there are harassment claims in the employment tribunals. These are linked to discrimination claims as they are based on an employee's protected characteristic. An employer will be guilty of harassment where they engage in unwanted conduct which has the purpose of effect of violating the employee's dignity or creating an intimidating, hostile, degrading, humiliating or offensive environment for that employee.

The need for medical experts in the employment tribunals

There has become a much greater need for medical evidence, particularly in disability discrimination cases. It is usually provided in the form of a written report by an independent medical expert. For example, the medical expert might need to report on whether the claimant is disabled. Therefore, a relevant impairment will need to be identified and whether it has a substantial adverse effect on the claimant's day-to-day activities. Also, whether the effect is minor and/or whether it is likely to become substantial and when the effect started and/or is likely to end. In relation to reasonable adjustments, a medical expert maybe asked to report on whether any particular reasonable adjustments would be effective in reducing or removing the disadvantage the claimant finds themselves at.

The need for medical evidence in disability discrimination cases for people with mental health issues was reinforced by the Employment Appeal Tribunal in the case of *Smiths Detection – Watford Ltd v Berriman UKEAT/0712/04* (a case involving the editor of this book at employment tribunal level) where His Honour Judge Serota QC said:

'In our opinion, as a general rule, in cases where a claimant's disability relates to his mental health, some medical evidence is likely to be required as to the effectiveness of any proposed adjustments. While a lay person does not need medical evidence to guide him as to the kind of adjustments than can be made to accommodate an employee in a wheelchair, even the most sophisticated employers are unlikely to have sufficient knowledge to enable them to devise, without expert assistance, adjustments to cope with an employee's mental health disabilities'.

Most importantly, the medical expert's report will be relevant to determining compensation for the claimant if they win their employment tribunal case; for example, the extent and likely length of any physical or psychological damage caused by the employer's failure to make reasonable adjustments. This is relevant to the award for injury to feelings and, in particular, injury to health. It may also be relevant to loss of earnings where the claimant feels unable to seek new employment. A claimant's compensation will be reduced if their health was deteriorating anyway, so even if reasonable adjustments had been made, they would not have been able to continue working for much longer. Also, their compensation will be reduced if they are in any way responsible for what had happened to them at work.

The choice of medical expert

A claimant can use a report by their own doctor, counsellor or consultant in employment tribunal claims. However, such reports will often have limited weight because of the potential risk of the doctor, counsellor or consultant not being impartial and/or being unrealistic with their prognosis. Therefore, the evidence of an independent medical expert is likely to be taken far more seriously by the employment tribunals as they will be regarded as more specialist and highly qualified than a doctor, counsellor or consultant and will also be viewed as more independent. The only drawback will be that the independent medical expert will not have been involved with the claimant from the start of their disability and/or the start of their trauma at work and will make their assessment of the claimant based on a single appointment.

The actual choice of medical expert will ultimately depend on the issues requiring evidence. Where there is a dispute as to whether the claimant meets the definition of disability, a consultant is often necessary. Where the issue relates to compensation, it will depend on the severity of the claimant's reactions. For example, if discrimination caused severe depression, posttraumatic stress disorder or a similar condition, evidence from a consultant psychiatrist would be usual.

Where it is a case of lesser injury to feelings, a GP may give evidence of the claimant's visits complaining of mild depression, sleeplessness etc. Usually a medical expert is required, but where the case concerns a mental impairment which is not an illness, e.g. dyslexia or learning difficulties, a report from a non-medical expert may be more appropriate, as long as they are suitably qualified e.g. an educational psychologist.

Employment tribunals - the procedure for obtaining medical evidence

Unlike in the civil courts, there is no -pre-action protocol applying to employment tribunal claims in respect of medical evidence. Further, a claimant does not, in principle, need to produce medical evidence in support of their claim at the outset although it will invariably be required in cases of disability discrimination and sex and race discrimination or harassment where the claimant alleges that they have suffered trauma at work.

In the absence of a pre-action protocol the usually way in which the employment tribunals approach the obtaining of medical evidence is to call the parties to a case management discussion at which it will be decided what type of medical evidence is required and the deadline by which the medical report must be disclosed. The employment tribunals prefer a joint expert to be instructed by the parties though it may be possible for the parties to instruct their own independent medical experts in which case the employment tribunal would be likely to order that the independent medical experts should meet after they have written their own reports and produce a joint statement. Where a joint expert is instructed, the letter of instruction will need to be agreed by the parties and included in the trial bundle for the (final) hearing along with the medical report itself.

In relation to the costs of medical reports, where the parties use their own independent medical experts then each side would pay the fees of their own independent medical experts. Where there is a joint expert, the parties would normally each pay half the fees. However, where the claimant is unable to afford those fees then the employment tribunal may be prepared to meet those fees or it may encourage the respondent to pay those fees.

The layout/format of a medico-legal report

A suggested format for an employment tribunal report is set out below:

a.   Title – Confidential Psychiatric Report on (name of claimant)

Report prepared at the request of (claimant's solicitors (and respondent's solicitors if joint report).

Prepared by (name of independent medical expert).

b.   Introduction:

-         Their qualifications.

-         Their brief in preparing the report.

-         Documents read in preparing the report.

c.   The claimant:

-         History of present complaint.

-         Personal and family history.

-         Medical history, medication - previous and current.

-         Examination including how the claimant came across during the examination and what tests were carried out.

d.   Diagnosis

e.   Treatment required

f.   Prognosis

g.   Opinion

h.   Statement of Truth (see below)

In particular, the requirements of the Civil Procedure Rules Part 35 (as used in all civil reports, e.g. personal injury) must be observed for the medico-legal report to be valid in the employment tribunal claim. Most importantly, the independent medical expert's report must be addressed to the employment tribunal and not to either of the parties. The report must be verified by the standard (civil proceedings) statement of truth in the following form:

'I confirm that I have made clear which facts and matters referred to in this report are within my own knowledge and which are not. Those that are within my own knowledge I confirm to be true. The opinions I have expressed represent my true and complete professional opinions on the matters to which they refer'.

Various standards of practice have been issued for medical expert witnesses. For example:

- The expert witness must be familiar with the Civil Procedure Rules Part 35 and will have knowledge of the medico-legal field
- The expert witness will provide advice and opinion only within their field of professional competence and expertise
- The expert witness will have effective communication and presentation skills
- The expert witness will practise in an ethical manner

- The expert witness will practise in a business-like manner and with integrity in managing their workload, keeping records and dealing with the financial aspects of the process

The independent medical expert would not normally be expected to attend the (final) hearing as their report would usually be accepted by the parties and in the event of any further clarification being required, the parties would normally address any further questions to the expert in writing. However, the expert should be prepared to attend the final hearing and be questioned.

Chapter 14 - The experts' meeting: narrowing the issues - **Laura Millman & Katherine Pearce**

Part 35.12 of the Civil Procedure Rules (CPR) governs meetings between experts. The purpose of expert meetings is to narrow the issues and, where possible, reach an agreed opinion on those issues. What is key, is to remember that your job is *not* to resolve or conclude the case, nor is it to agree what you think a judge should decide; your sole reason for being there is to identify what is in agreement and what is not. In our experience we have found the following key points to be helpful when thinking about the expert meeting and how best to approach it - but remember to always refer back to the CPR if in any doubt as to the purpose of the expert meeting.

Be prepared

We cannot stress strongly enough how important it is to scrutinise everything that you have been provided with, including documentation from the other side. You should note similarities and differences in how you view the case, as opposed to how your opposite number does, in terms of both the evidence and in how you reached your conclusions. This means going through the medical records provided, all statements and reports you have received and any disclosed reports or literature from the other side. It may be that the other expert is relying upon literature you have not seen. In this case, you should ensure you are provided with this information and consider it ahead of the meeting. We have had an expert who, unfortunately, was not sufficiently prepared and at the meeting was ambushed with literature from the other side that, although disclosed, was not considered. This may not collapse the case, but it is not a position you would want to find yourself in.

An agenda is usually agreed between the solicitors for each side before the meeting takes place. You should expect your instructing solicitor to provide you with a draft agenda for you to consider and amend if necessary. If they have not done so, you ought to request the draft agenda before it is agreed to ensure you are content with not only the questions being asked, but also the way in which the questions have been framed.

Once you have reviewed the draft agenda and made your suggestions, it will normally be sent to the other side and the same process will be undertaken with their expert. Whilst there may be a bit of give and take, there should ultimately be nothing in the agreed agenda that surprises you. You should address any issues in the agenda before it is agreed to ensure that you are entirely happy with it.

Lawyers like to wrangle with each other about the format of questions in the agenda – often one solicitor will insist on a specific wording which may in fact already be addressed but worded slightly differently by the other side. In this situation, you need to consider the core issue that is being addressed and ensure that you answer consistently at the meeting. There are instances when a draft agenda cannot be agreed and you end up with two agendas. This is probably because solicitors are trying to control the discussion! If you find yourself in this situation, you should answer the questions contained in both agendas, ensuring that you are consistent in both and remember that the purpose of the meeting is to narrow the issues; to determine what is in agreement and what is not.

Before the meeting, ensure you have familiarised yourself with the issues in the case and be clear on the areas of your evidence where there will be no compromise and areas where there may be. If your opinion is beginning to waiver, tell your instructing solicitor prior to the meeting and they can advise how best to manage it. Ahead of the meeting, ensure you are content with the venue itself and the availability of necessary technology (laptop, internet connection etc.) to allow you to properly discuss the issues.

The meeting itself

You find yourself face to face with your mentor at the expert meeting; so what do you do? What is key is that you do not get ambushed or feel intimidated. It may be that you are sitting opposite someone who has been your senior or someone who has taught you at some stage of your academic career. This is obviously not an easy place to be, but if you are prepared you should be in a good position to stand your ground and not feel swayed. Remember your views are based on a balanced approach; you will have considered the opposing opinions and found in favour of your view, substantiated with literature and evidence. Stand your ground and believe in yourself. Do not feel the need to be defensive - be objective and assertive.

There is provision in the CPR for instructing solicitors to be present at the meeting but it is widely felt that this inhibits free and frank discussion. If solicitors do attend they are not permitted to intervene in the discussions, other than to advise on the law. If your instructing solicitor informs you he or she is attending the expert meeting, you may wish to take a view on whether you consider it appropriate and advise them accordingly.

You should not feel obliged to reach compromise or agreement at the meeting - that is the court's job (as you should already be aware, from previous chapters). There may be situations where issues are raised by your opposite number that you have not previously considered. This may be in the form of unexplained theories or views, or indeed new theories and opinions. This may present a dichotomy but do not feel you need to find a new way of viewing the case that encapsulates the opinions of both you and your opposite number. You need to be categoric and consistent in your opinion. If you cannot be, do not answer. If you find you are veering from the agenda, beware! A 'no comment' response is entirely acceptable and certainly preferable to muddying the waters by highlighting a new analysis or theory. It is unhelpful to your instructing solicitor if you suddenly move your position based on new information that has arisen in the meeting. If this situation arises, provide a 'no comment' response and advise your instructing solicitor after the meeting to allow them to deal with this. If, in the course of your discussions in the meeting, issues are raised that do not relate to items on the agenda but are relevant to the case, you can advise on what action should be taken to address this. This is permitted by the CPR. You should consider the implications of any new issues, identify why they are relevant to the case and, again, determine whether you agree or disagree with your opposite number.

The meeting will undoubtedly contain a discussion about the facts of the case and a possible range of opinions and views - you would not be at the meeting if you and the other expert had come to the same conclusion in your reports! Remember you are relating the issues in discussion to the legal tests and not to medical certainty. The discussion should result in a statement phrased, whether agreed or disagreed, using the terminology of legal tests, be it breach of duty, causation or both. It may also be appropriate for the discussion to address issues of fact that can be agreed between you and the other expert. If this is the case, these should be included in the statement. Throughout the meeting remember that your role is to narrow the issues in dispute and if possible come to a conclusion with your opposite number as to what you agree or disagree on.

The joint statement

After the meeting, a joint statement will be prepared and agreed between you and your opposite number. There are timescales dictated by the Civil Procedure Rules that will be reiterated in the court's directions. You need to agree and sign the joint statement within 7 days of the meeting and provide it to your instructing solicitor within 14 days after signing. When reviewing the joint statement, remember to review the questions in the agenda and anticipate how they may be interpreted by the court or a barrister in cross-examination. If in doubt, amend the statement to ensure that you are entirely happy with it.

Remember that the joint statement should answer the questions prepared in the agenda or, as the case may be, the agendas, and not contain the discussions at the meeting. If the scenario arises where you have been presented with information that has gone beyond the questions, do not be afraid to provide a 'no comment' as your response. However, if new issues relevant to the case were raised in the meeting, the statement should include these issues and make it clear what your advice is and whether you agree or disagree on the specific points. The statement needs to reflect what has been agreed or disagreed during the course of your discussions and nothing more. Make sure you alert your instructing solicitors to any new issues so they can resolve them with the other side's solicitors.

You have time to agree the joint statement - you should not feel under pressure to agree it but reflect back to the points above and remember the purpose of the meeting. Read through the statement to ensure that you have been consistent throughout. Consider your terminology and the legal test - words such as 'most', 'possible' and 'may' create ambiguity which is the worst-case scenario for those involved - except counsel who will exploit any such ambiguity in cross-examination.

Think back to how you expressed your opinion in your report and, as you did then, use categoric language in your answers that will satisfy the legal tests. You need to trust why you came to the conclusion you did in the first place but if you feel less sure of your opinion, address your concerns with your instructing solicitor before agreeing and signing the joint statement. If you have agreed the statement and after such agreement it emerges that you are unhappy with the meaning it confers, thereby creating a question in relation to the credibility of your evidence, it is possible for you to produce a corrected statement but ultimately this weakens your expert opinion. It is far better to be comfortable with the agreed statement in the first place and avoid such a situation. Again, if in doubt contact your instructing solicitor before finalising the statement.

Conclusion

The expert meeting can play a key part in the case and a well prepared, consistent and categoric joint statement will be central to narrowing the issues in dispute and may result in settlement of the case. Your role is important, so remember to be prepared. Remember the purpose of the meeting is to narrow the issues, not to conclude the case. Stand your ground and make sure you keep your solicitor informed of any wavering.

Chapter 15 - How to answer questions in court - Shamsun Nahar

Introduction

Giving expert evidence in court requires a high standard of accuracy and impartiality. The importance of fulfilling this obligation properly can be summarised by four key factors. Firstly, as with all expert reports, psychiatric reports comprise the *opinion* of the author. It follows that the opinions submitted in a report and subsequently recited in court are likely to be subjected to robust testing. This is particularly the case when parties instruct psychiatrists with differing opinions which can result in vigorous cross examination. Secondly, opinions must be confined to the knowledge of the expert and there should not be a departure from this. Thirdly, the evidence of an expert is likely to have more influence than that of an ordinary witness. Fourthly, it is fundamental to remember that the primary duty of an expert witness is to the court. This means being truthful as to fact, comprehensive in reasoning, and thorough in consideration of relevant matters. These features apply to written evidence as well as oral evidence on oath. The Criminal Procedure Rules 2012 require that 'an expert must help the court to achieve the overriding objective by giving objective, unbiased opinion on matters within his expertise'. This is no less so in civil or family law. With this background, the current chapter will focus on how to answer questions in court.

Examination in chief

After taking the oath, questions on experience and qualifications will be raised to ascertain the witness' position as an expert, and essentially to allow opinion evidence. It is usual for the preliminary part of this evidence to be adduced through leading questions, and often the expert's CV is read out in court so that credentials can be confirmed. It is worth noting that whether the witness is proficient to give evidence as an expert is ultimately a matter for the court to resolve.

Once the credibility of the expert is established, examination in chief will follow. Questions will be put to adduce the evidence contained within the report and importantly, the conclusions contained within the report will be drawn out. A fundamental consideration when answering questions in examination in chief is that if a question is asked which is outside the field of expertise of a psychiatrist, the question should not be answered and the court informed.

Cross examination

It will be presumed that the other side have accepted the evidence, if there is no cross examination to indicate that the evidence is not agreed. Accordingly, the purpose of cross examination is to weaken the other side's case. There are a number of ways this can be achieved, from attacking the reliability or knowledge of the expert, to seeking to get the expert to contradict their testimony. To that end, and as mentioned above, the expert should be mindful that questions may be asked which encourage an opinion outside the field of expertise of a psychiatrist. Attempts may also be made to support the other side's case by bringing out evidence which corroborates it. It is fundamental when answering questions under cross examination that the question asked is addressed, and not to forecast or anticipate what is behind it. By avoiding speculation and answering questions in one's own words, credibility will be maintained.

Re-examination

This is limited to a clarification of matters arising out of cross examination, and no fresh facts may be introduced without the leave of the court. In general, leading questions are not permissible in re-examination.

Giving evidence

Prior to giving evidence the expert report will have been disclosed and served on the opposing party as well as the court. This allows the other party to consider the report and instruct their own psychiatric expert to prepare a report to support their case. If the reports reach differing conclusions, it is likely that both experts will be required to give evidence in court. It is worth noting that in certain circumstances, evidence may be given by a single joint expert. Either way, whilst giving evidence the report may be referred to if necessary to refresh the memory. When giving evidence, the below points will assist in answering questions competently in court:

- Dress in business attire to look professional and ensure that one's demeanour inspires confidence
- Remember the overriding duty to the court and provide truthful, unbiased answers
- The ultimate aim is to provide answers in a well-executed and well-presented manner
- Make statements concisely and clearly. When referring to technical issues, explain the concept in the simplest

terms so that it is understood by lay persons. The jury (if present) need to understand the significance of the evidence

- Speak slowly. A note will be made of the evidence, therefore it is useful to watch the judge's pen to determine whether the pace is correct
- Answer questions with a "yes" or "no" where no further statement is warranted
- Where further explanation is necessary, answer in a straightforward manner but keep the answer short
- When technical terminology is used, explain the meaning of the terms in a manner which is not confusing
- Listen carefully to the question and answer the specific question. This may sound simple but even expert witnesses, if not concentrating can answer the question they expect to be asked rather than the question itself
- Avoid offering more detail than what is required. If further information is required, this will be made clear
- If fresh evidence or counter arguments are put forward during the course of questioning, opinions may need to be modified. In such circumstances flexibility in thinking will assist

- Do not feel embarrassed to ask for clarification or ask for a question to be repeated.

- Make eye contact with the person asking questions but answers should be addressed to the jury (if present) or the judge

- One's voice should be modulated so answers are heard by everyone in court

- Never give a sarcastic answer. Answers must be professional at all times

- As with all witnesses, experts should be given the opportunity to finish answers. If interrupted, ask (the judge) for the opportunity to finish answering

- Once the oath has been taken, evidence should not be discussed with anyone. In exceptional circumstances, the court may give permission to discuss matters about which the expert has not yet given evidence

- It is permissible to draw on the work of other expert psychiatrists in reaching a conclusion, provided the material is referred to during evidence

- Avoid opinion on the general merits of the case unless specifically asked

Conclusion

In order to proficiently answer questions in court, as well as adopting the points mentioned above, it is beneficial for expert psychiatrists to have a sound comprehension of the subject matter in dispute. Analytical reasoning will be essential when answering questions in court, as will the ability to communicate opinions and findings clearly and concisely. To deal effectively with cross examination it will be necessary to think on one's feet, without forgetting the overriding duty to the court and without bias towards the party responsible for payment of fees. After answering questions in court, the overall impression of the evidence should be that the evidence is independent and unbiased.

Chapter 16 - The loss of expert immunity - how to protect against being sued - **Leslie Keegan**

Introduction

The courts have been assisted by medical experts since at least as early as 1345, when surgeons were summoned to court to opine on the freshness of a wound (Rix, 2006). The courts have admitted psychiatric evidence since at least the 18th century, when Dr John Monro gave evidence at the trial of Lord Ferrers, who had shot his former steward in a fit of temper and pleaded insanity (R v. Ferrers). However, it is in only in very recent times that the immunity from suit that was afforded to expert witnesses has been stripped away and it is clear that expert witnesses can now be sued for providing negligent expert evidence, just as they could previously be sued for negligently providing any other service. It was not surprising that, given the increasing trend towards providing redress for those who suffer an injustice or other harm, this was going to happen. However, in order to understand the implications of this recent radical change it is helpful to look at the important role of witnesses historically and in particular expert witnesses in the legal process and to consider why there was such reluctance to strip away the immunity from suit that was afforded to experts.

All witnesses are an essential part of the legal process, providing factual or opinion evidence. The court's powers to exercise legal sanctions and to apply legal rules clearly depend on the proof of particular facts. The law establishes which facts have to be proven in any given case, by whom and to what standard of proof. These facts are proven by evidence, usually by oral evidence but also by documentary evidence and real evidence (which is derived from the physical nature of an object or place and observed upon an examination or visit).

What are the burden and the standard of proof?

The burden of proof refers to the legal duty imposed upon a civil or criminal defendant to prove or disprove a disputed fact. In a criminal case, the burden of proof is placed on the prosecution which has to demonstrate to the jury that a defendant is guilty, whereas in a civil case the burden of proof is placed on the claimant who has to demonstrate to the judge's satisfaction that the case that he or she asserts is right. The standard of proof refers to the fact that every allegation in a case must be established to a particular standard; the standard of proof for criminal cases is 'beyond reasonable doubt' and the standard of proof for civil cases is on the balance of probabilities'.

What is the role of a witness?

The court will receive evidence of fact from a witness for consideration in a case. The evidence of a factual witness is usually presented by the witness attending court, going into the witness box, swearing an oath or affirming, then giving his or her evidence orally to the court. In England and Wales, the courts' rules of procedure also allow for reliance on written, sworn witness statements in place of calling a witness to give evidence orally. In Scotland, such statements have to be given on oath before a commissioner appointed by the court, and are only permitted in circumstances where the witness is unable to attend court due to circumstances such as ill health, old age or a requirement to be abroad when the case is heard in court. By contrast, in Northern Ireland, it is very rare for statements to be accepted in place of oral evidence. Each statement of fact by the witness is evidence of that fact, and once the evidence has been 'given' on oath or affirmation, it becomes 'sworn evidence' or 'testimony'.

Difference between evidence of fact and opinion evidence

Opinions and conclusions are for the court to reach based upon its assessment of the information placed before it; its factual conclusions should be based upon the evidence of fact put before it. Its legal conclusions will be based on its application of the law to the facts it has found, having regard to the legal arguments put before it by the advocates and consequently the opinions of lay witnesses are not generally admissible as evidence in court. This is called 'the rule against opinion evidence'.

The main exception to the general rule excluding evidence of a witness's opinion is in respect of 'expert evidence' given by an expert witness. This opinion evidence is received when the court requires additional assistance to decide justly a particular issue which concerns matters of specialised knowledge and expertise. A medical expert is usually called to give expert evidence in cases in which instance they will be giving an interpretation of the facts of the case. This opinion evidence may be admitted provided the court is satisfied that the witness is qualified to give that opinion by relevant learning and experience.

Traditionally, there was immunity from suit for witnesses. The immunity from suit as set out by the Court of Appeal in the case of Stanton v Callaghan dates back over 400 years to a case known as Cutler v Dixon (1585). In this case the reason given by the court for rejecting the claim was that if such actions were allowed then those who have just cause for complaint would be deterred from complaining for fear of infinite vexation. The immunity dates back to a time long before the modern law of negligence was established and it also dates back to a time long before it became commonplace for forensic experts to offer their services under contract for reward. The principle thinking behind this was that witnesses should be able to give their evidence free from worry that they might be sued. Kelly CB in the case of Dawkins v Lord Rokeby in 1873 stated that witnesses before tribunals recognised by law should be able to 'give their testimony free from any fear of being harassed by an action on an allegation, whether true or false, that they acted from malice'.

In the case of Darker v Chief Constable of West Midlands Lord Hutton in 2001 approved of these comments by CB Kelly. The issue in the case of Darker was whether witness immunity extended to protect police officers who were alleged to have fabricated evidence from claims of conspiracy to injure and misfeasance in public office. The claimants had been indicted for serious offences but their trial had been permanently stayed on the grounds of abuse of process on the part of the police. Their lordships identified the following reasons for witness immunity: to protect witnesses who have given evidence in good faith, to encourage honest and well-meaning persons to assist just and to ensure that the witness will speak freely and fearlessly.

What did the immunity extend to traditionally?

In order to understand the issue it is helpful to consider what the immunity extended to and what it did not extend to:

- The preliminary examination of witnesses and statements made in relation to the proceedings attracted immunity from suit privilege
- Statements and reports *before* civil proceedings were covered by immunity
- Statements and reports prepared in circumstances where if there were to be proceedings for child abuse the report would be relied upon

- Statements made out of court that could fairly said to be part of the investigative process of investigating a crime with a view to prosecution

The immunity did not protect somebody, however, where there were things done at investigation stage, which could *not* fairly be said to be part of the investigative process.

The immunity of expert witnesses persisted for so long because it was seen as promoting two objectives. Firstly, it ensured that experts could give evidence without fear of being sued and secondly, it avoided a multiplicity of actions.

Could expert immunity really persist in light of other changes?

There were a number of changes which indicated that the time for the immunity from suit for expert witnesses was coming to an end. There were three particular cases involving the immunity from suit for barristers and where the change in approach of the courts in those cases indicated the way that the wind was blowing. The difference in approach of the court between the cases of Rondel and the cases of Saif Ali and

Hall indicated that the time for expert' s immunity from suit was also likely to come to an end.

The case of Rondel v Worsley concerned a barrister's immunity in relation to things done *in court* and the immunity was upheld on three grounds: -

- The administration of justice required that a barrister should be able to carry out his duty to the court fearlessly and independently
- Actions for negligence would make re-trying of the original actions inevitable and so prolong litigation, contrary to public interest
- The cab-rank rule, by which a barrister is obliged to accept any client who sought his or her services.

It is clear that the thinking at that time was that allowing barristers to be sued would affect their ability to take on risky cases and to pursue these fearlessly and independently and that it would lead to re-trying of actions and prolonged litigation. However, when the House of Lords in 1980 came to look at the issue again it was perfectly clear that there were the beginnings of a change in approach.

In the case of Saif Ali v Sidney Mitchell a barrister had settled claim documents and advised on the issue in dispute. The House of Lords held by a bare majority that the barrister would not be immune on the basis that it was only pre-trial works so intimately connected with the conduct of the hearing of the case in court, would be immune.

In 2002 there was further erosion of the protection of barristers from immunity. In the case of Arthur JS Hall & Co v Simons, the House of Lords held that given the changes in society and in the law that have taken place since the decision in Rondel it was appropriate to review the public policy decision that advocates enjoyed immunity from liability for the negligent conduct of a case in court. The propriety of maintaining such immunity depended upon the balance between, on the one hand, the normal right of an individual to be compensated for a legal wrong done to him and, on the other, the advantages which accrued to the public interest from such immunity.

The court decided that in relation to claims for immunity for an advocate in civil proceedings, such balance no longer showed sufficient public benefit as to justify the maintenance of the immunity of the advocate. The decision was that immunity should be abolished in relation to all proceedings, and not merely in relation to the conduct of civil proceedings.

The case of Professor Sir Roy Meadow before the GMC (General Medical Council) focused intense media and public, as well as professional, attention on the role of the medical expert. He had given evidence in the murder trial of Sally Clarke who was convicted of the murder of her first two children. Sally Clarke's second appeal against conviction was allowed by the Court of Appeal on the basis of a failure (not by Prof Meadow) to disclose significant microbiological results. Professor Meadow had given evidence about the statistical chances of two cot deaths occurring in the one family but it was alleged he failed to explain the limited significance of the statistic.

The Fitness to Practise Panel accepted that he had not intended to mislead but was 'an eminent paediatrician whose reputation was renowned throughout the world'. His eminence and authority, which gave the misleading evidence such great weight, carried with it a unique responsibility to take meticulous care in a case of this grave nature. Initially he was found guilty of serious professional misconduct by the GMC but he was exonerated by the High Court, which found that, although his evidence was flawed it was honestly given. He did not intend to mislead the court and his uncharacteristic and honest error fell far short of serious professional misconduct. The Court of Appeal upheld that decision.

However, there were indications of the reluctance of courts to hold experts liable for their reports as shown by the decision in the case of Stanton v Callaghan. Prior to Jones v Kaney (see below) this case was the leading case on the immunity conferred in respect of a claim brought by a litigant against his own expert witness. The defendant was a structural engineer instructed as an expert by the plaintiffs in a claim brought against insurers in relation to subsidence at the plaintiffs' house. The expert's initial opinion was that total underpinning of the house was required at a cost of some £77,000. In the course of preparing a joint report with the insurers' expert he agreed that infilling with polystyrene at a cost of £21,000 would be adequate. The case was settled on that basis but the plaintiffs then brought a claim against their expert arguing that their expert's change of advice had been negligent. The Master refused to strike out the claim but on appeal the Court of Appeal reversed the decision.

The Court of Appeal summarised the effect of the previous authorities and stated that an expert witness who gives evidence at trial is immune from suit in respect of anything he says in court and that immunity extended to the contents of the report which he adopts as his evidence. His conclusion was that the public interest in preserving immunity was required in order to avoid the tension between a desire to assist the court and the fear of consequences of a departure from previous advice.

In the Stanton v Callaghan case the Court of Appeal approved Cresswell J's definition of the duties of an expert as set out in the Ikarian Reefer case:

- The report should be the independent product of the expert uninfluenced by the pressures of litigation
- The expert should provide independent assistance to the court by way of objective unbiased opinion
- The expert should state the facts and assumptions upon which the report is based
- The expert should make it clear if something is outside of his or her expertise
- The report should make it clear if the opinion is qualified because of having insufficient data

- If the expert changes his or her mind having seen the other side's report he or she should let the other side and the court know
- If the opinion is based on photos, plans or measurements the expert should make these available to other side at time of the exchange of reports

These duties are now set out in the 'Protocol for the Instruction of Experts to give Evidence in Civil Claims'.

When the expert attended the meeting with his opposite number he enjoyed immunity. The purpose of the joint meeting, to identify areas of agreement and disagreement, was in the public interest. It was considered that the duty to the court must override the fear of suit arising out of a departure from a previously held position.

However, as had been expected by some, given the removal of immunity from suit that barristers previously enjoyed, the Supreme Court has now removed the partial immunity from suit for negligence previously enjoyed by expert witnesses. In the case of Jones v Kaney (see below) the Supreme Court found that expert witnesses can now be sued for providing negligent expert evidence just as they could be sued for negligently providing any other service. It should be noted however, that in his dissenting judgment in Jones , Lord Hope pointed out that nobody who had sat in the case of Arthur JS Hall & Co v Simons (see above) foresaw that removing the immunity from suit for advocates would be taken as an indication that it should be removed from expert witnesses too.

The case of Paul Wynne Jones v Sue Kaney, followed on from Ms Kaney giving expert evidence in a road traffic accident. The defendant, Ms Kaney, was an expert witness in the case. She was instructed as a psychology expert. In the course of the litigation, she met with the defendant's psychology expert. The agreed joint statement of the experts turned out to be very critical of the claimant.

Two extracts from that joint statement indicate that it was very damaging to the claimant's prospects of success in recovering damages for his head injury in the road traffic claim. At paragraph 4, under the heading 'Diagnosis' it recorded 'Both experts agree that Mr Jones' psychological reaction, after the accident, was no more than an adjustment reaction that did not reach the level of a psychiatric disorder of either a depressive disorder, or posttraumatic stress disorder'.

At paragraph 5 it recorded: 'Dr Kaney has found Mr Wynne Jones to be very deceptive and deceitful in his reporting. He denied any previous psychological trouble or past accidents, which is inconsistent with the records or other reports. Despite enquiry he did not report to her the other road traffic accident of 28.02.2001. We therefore agree that such inconsistencies would be suggestive of conscious mechanisms and would raise doubts of whether his subjective reporting was genuine'.

The solicitors for Paul Wynne Jones, the claimant, investigated with the defendant, Ms Kaney, why she had allegedly changed her opinion so radically and on what basis she had found the claimant to be very deceptive and deceitful in his reporting. Her answers in correspondence and telephone conversations, suggested an unhappy picture of how that joint statement came to be signed. However, one must stress that these allegations have not been tested, much less fully explored yet by any court, and are contested by Dr Kaney. They may be summarised as follows:

- She had not seen the reports of the opposing expert at the time of the telephone conference
- The joint statement, as drafted by the opposing expert, did not reflect what she had agreed in the telephone

conversation, but she had felt under some pressure in agreeing it

- Her true view was that the claimant had been evasive rather than deceptive
- It was her view that the claimant did suffer posttraumatic stress disorder which was now resolved
- She was happy for the claimant's then solicitors to amend the joint statement

The court at first instance considered that the court and the Court of Appeal were bound by Stanton v Callaghan but granted a certificate for a 'leap-frog appeal' to the Supreme Court. Expert witnesses have lost their immunity from being sued over matters arising in the course of proceedings, following this landmark ruling by the Supreme Court.

Lord Hope and Lady Hale provided the dissenting judgments in the Jones v Kaney case and their judgments provided some indications of the difficulties that may arise by the decision. Lord Hope pointed out that the decision does nothing to define what is meant by an expert witness. Lord Hope cited the examples of the joint or court appointed expert. He also cited those who, although not experts, can be said to owe a duty to a party to the litigation or to a party who may be affected by what they say. He referred to the company director who owes a duty of care to the company to promote its interests but makes an inexcusable error when giving evidence or the skilled employee who gives evidence and is said to have done so negligently, causing loss to his employer.

Lady Hale followed Lord Hope in setting out the difficulties which the abolition of immunity would create. She pointed out that the argument advanced on behalf of the claimant was that the expert here was called in to give an opinion for the purpose of the litigation, was paid a fee for doing so and would ordinarily owe a contractual duty to exercise reasonable care and skill and if they failed to exercise that they should be held liable. She clarified that the argument advanced was that in these circumstances the experts should be held liable if they failed the Bolam test (of what a 'reasonable body of medical men' would do). She suggested that caution had to be exercised - if the law was changed to abolish the immunity of experts from suit it must be done in a principled way as it would apply between expert witnesses and their clients in all sorts of civil proceedings.

She stated that although the above may sound straightforward, even in ordinary civil cases, it is not always so. A doctor who treated a patient after an accident or for an industrial disease may be called upon to give evidence not only of what happened, but also in relation to the future. Sometimes a fee was involved and sometimes not. She raised the question as to whether it was proposed that the exception would cover all or only part of their evidence. She pointed out that the cases involving psychiatrists who are instructed on behalf of patients in tribunal proceedings under the Mental Health Act 1983 involve sensitive and often highly fraught cases in which performing a duty to the tribunal may well be perceived by the client patient as a breach of duty towards him or her. Furthermore, in public law family proceedings involving a local authority, the child and the parents there is often a great deal of expert evidence. Some of the evidence comes from social workers employed by the local authority, some of these are simple witnesses of fact while some will have carried out expert risk assessments and many will have done both. She posed the question as to whether they would be liable to the local authority in respect of some or all of their actions.

She also gave the example of the case of D v East Berkshire Community NHS Trust where the Court of Appeal held that both doctors and social workers owed a duty of care to the child when conducting child protection investigations. In that case, Lord Phillips MR (Master of the Rolls) stated that it may not be easy to draw the line between investigation and the preparation of evidence in cases of suspected child abuse but the court clearly held that is where the line should be drawn. Lady Hale stated that these examples make clear that in many family cases, if the law was changed, there would be some professional witnesses who enjoy immunity in respect of their evidence and some who did not. She said that it was not self-evident that the policy considerations in favour of making the change in the law were so strong that the Supreme Court should depart from their previous authority. She opined that it was 'self-evidently' a topic more suitable for consideration by the Law Commission and reform , if thought appropriate, should be by Parliament rather than by the Supreme Court. Nevertheless, the Supreme Court, by a majority, went on to make the change in the law and remove the immunity from suit for expert witnesses.

What can experts do to protect themselves from being sued?

Although the precise subtleties of the decision in Jones v Kaney may take some time to discover there are some clear implications of the decision. The first, and most important, of these is that expert witnesses should make sure that they have professional indemnity cover or insurance which specifically includes their activities as an expert witness. There is also the question as to whether expert witnesses will seek to limit or exclude their liability by contractual terms. Such limitation or exclusion would need to comply with the relevant legislation on contractual fairness to be effective. However, clients are unlikely to be willing to accept exclusions of liability, but may be more willing to accept limitations of liability to the extent of a reasonable amount of insurance cover that may be available.

There are also some things that experts can, and should, do to improve the quality of a report and to avoid being criticised. The first thing is to request a paginated and indexed copy of the medical records and statements. Even if provided with a chronology, it is advisable to prepare your own - it is both a useful tool for concentrating the mind on relevant events and helps the reader understand what happened when. In preparing the chronology it is helpful to include information not just from the clinical notes but also information from referral letters, discharge summaries and any nursing notes, remembering that the written nursing notes often contain information which is not available elsewhere.

Whether one is dealing with civil, criminal or family proceedings, as anyone who has read this book thus far must be all too aware, the overriding duty of the doctor preparing a report is to the court, and not to any of the parties such as the claimant, the prosecution, the defence, or a patient. This contrasts with the primary responsibility in clinical care, where the primary duty is to the patient. The role is to provide an objective, unbiased opinion on matters within the expertise of the expert, and one should never assume the role of an advocate on behalf of the instructing party.

It occasionally happens that an expert is asked to prepare a report on the basis of very limited information such as a telephone call, a few witness statements or incomplete records. Requests to prepare reports cases without access to vital materials, such as the complete medical records, should always be treated with great caution; any report, or opinion, expressed on the basis of incomplete information should always make clear its limitations. It is an absolute obligation on the expert to make it clear if a question falls outside his or her particular expertise or if insufficient information has been provided to answer any question completely.

It requires constant vigilance and professionalism to avoid bias creeping into a report. Selective extraction of negative information is one of the most common faults in medical reports. It is important to keep in mind at all times that the expert's overriding duty, in preparing a report, is to the court. It is a mistake to comment on an area that is outside one's area of expertise; again something which anyone who has read the book thus far should be well aware of. An expert must have sufficient practical experience in the area. Lawyers sometimes have a poor understanding of the different areas of medical expertise, and the onus is clearly on the expert to politely but firmly state when a question or issue is outside one's area of expertise. The temptation to try to be helpful and 'have a stab' at the question must be resisted. By all means suggest a colleague who may be better placed to help, but it is not the expert's responsibility to find such a person.

It may be relevant to refer to medical literature. What is not acceptable is to selectively provide a few references that bolster the point of view that you wish to advance, while ignoring all material that points in other directions. The volume of medical literature is such that one can usually find some articles to support almost any point of view, however outrageous.

However, the court needs a balanced assessment of the evidence.

When writing a report, one may feel (or actually be placed) under considerable pressure to express an undue degree of boldness and confidence, for fear that to do otherwise may weaken the case for the instructing party. However, the expert is under an obligation to point out any limitations of his or her report. Where there is a range of opinion the expert must summarise this and give reasons for their own opinion. If one is not able to give an opinion without qualification, the qualification must be stated. Through no fault on the part of the expert, there may be all sorts of limitations; certain information may have been unavailable, or other reports or information may be awaited. The expert should state any such limitations clearly as it is of assistance to the court to understand that he or she has recognised and acknowledged that the report may be limited due to certain factors.

If, following the preparation of a report, on reflection, the expert realises that he or she arrived at an incorrect conclusion; it is a strength and not a weakness, to readily acknowledge this. It is a common experience at experts' meetings that opinions change when the experts have a chance to understand the reasoning of a colleague, or when an expert learns of new facts of which they were unaware. Experts who change their opinions for good reason on receipt of fresh information are respected by the court, rather than criticised. However, any change of opinion must always be fully explained and one should be prepared to defend one's rationale.

Chapter 17 - Experts - the trainee's viewpoint - **Sam Vhondo**

Duties of an expert witness

It is arguable that legal practitioners can take a few guiding principles from legal trainees when it comes to instructing expert witnesses. Trainees are a 'fresh pair of eyes' so they are able to identify the omitted points that could benefit courtroom efficiency. The question is not of fact; most expert witnesses are established professionals in their field. However, do they have the practical tools to be of assistance in court? The practical tools necessary to validate the work done by expert witnesses are arguably not easily recognised. This chapter looks at these specific areas in an attempt to assist the aspiring psychiatric expert witness.

Basic factors

There are some basic factors that could be considered trivial by practitioners; however they may have a large impact on the case. It is important to get an accurate and chronological measure of date and time of incident in order to clarify the events of the case. With regard to the mental health field issues of diagnosis are important. All the expert witnesses should be able to interpret clearly the main diagnosis to the court. They ought to be able to explain the rationale of their conclusions and confirm whether the symptoms experienced by the client are conclusive evidence of their diagnosis. Practically it is also important to gauge the significant factors of the said incident in order to come to an accurate conclusion. For example, the mental state of the claimant during the time of incident should be questioned. Influences such as stress, drug intoxication or the symptoms of the illness at the time of incident ought to be raised.

Qualities required of an expert witness

It is imperative that all expert reports be independent, objective and unbiased. In order to achieve this, all expert witnesses need to have a sound knowledge of the subject matter in contention. This can be achieved through a thorough assessment of the merits of each given case on a preliminary basis before agreeing to provide a report. They need to be able to make a differentiation between personal opinion and fact. The expert witness needs to have sufficient analytical reasoning skills to fulfil their obligations to the court. This can only be achieved if they are both well informed about their subject matter and any professional issues (important in clinical negligence cases). One way to stay informed is to continuously update their knowledge, not only with current thinking and any significant developments within their field, but also within the legal field affecting their expert witness work.

Arguably, it is expected that expert witnesses may refer to theories written by eminent fellow practitioners when making their case. However, they must utilise as much information given to them as possible. If they have very little information to go on, experts should strongly advocate to the instructing parties for all records to be given to them prior to rendering a final opinion. Potential expert witnesses need not agree to take on cases unless given an opportunity to make a thorough review of the medical records relevant to the case. All the while it is advisable for the expert to adopt a demeanour that is likely to inspire confidence, particularly during court appearances.

It is vital for expert witnesses to communicate their findings in a clear and concise manner. This is applicable in both written reports and oral testimony. If done carelessly this could lead to misinterpretation of facts. It is important that when giving evidence, all the illustrations and examples are clear, relevant and free of riddles or professional 'lingo'. The expert needs to pay attention to their use of language and avoid the use of vague statements with potential double meanings and focus on the facts.

Given that law is a subject that is continuously evolving, expert witnesses need to have the flexibility of mind in order to modify opinions in the light of fresh evidence or counter arguments. This skill is especially important during cross-examining of experts. Therefore, they need to be able to 'think on their feet', so as to cope with intense periods of cross-examination.

Professionalism

In terms of qualifications and experience, expert witnesses should make it clear how far their experience (and therefore expertise) stretches. It is pointless for a solicitor to instruct an expert witness qualified to advise on only a limited number of matters in dispute unless it is evident that there are disparate areas which require one than one expert. Being clear about your limitations helps the solicitor to ensure that the right expert is chosen. When making assertions expert witnesses ought to ensure that they are utilising relevant and appropriate tools to reach an appropriate conclusion. This is especially important to those experts who rely heavily on unqualified assistance. They should minimise their reliance on unqualified assistance when making their final conclusions. This will ensure that their report is not susceptible to mistakes.

It is only through experience that the expert witness can understand the importance of boundaries and the importance of only concentrating on relevant matters. For example boundaries ought to be set to ensure that it is predominantly the individual's account which they base their conclusions on unless they can clearly demonstrate that some other source is more authoritative (e.g. the medical notes). Although mostly helpful, opinion from family members may sometimes prove a hindrance, especially if undue weight is put upon it. The relevant issues that need emphasis are not always obvious to the inexperienced eye. Sometimes more balanced reports flow from the experience of testifying in court and hearing the views of both sides being put to the expert. The experience that the psychiatrist gathers in the witness box helps them develop as a well-respected expert.

Confidentiality and conflict of interest

Law touches on sensitive issues that require a high level of professionalism. Therefore, expert witnesses need to be mindful of the risks involved when acting in cases involving former patients. These could produce conflicts of interest. It is also necessary to tread carefully in order to avoid cross-referencing confidential matters from other cases, if the expert has been involved in more than arena of law. The key is, whether the expert opinion is independent of both parties and the pressures of litigation. If a potential conflict arises, the expert witness should seek guidance from professional advisors and/or (both sets of) instructing solicitors before agreeing to act. However, ultimately the obligation is on the expert with any potential conflict of interest to disclose the details at an early stage of the proceedings. This will give the other party and the court an opportunity to assess the conflict to see if they are content with it. Even in the absence of any perceived conflict, if a psychiatrist is treating a patient who is involved in proceedings they must consent for the psychiatrist to produce a report. If they do not the psychiatrist ought to decline instructions in the case.

Ethical considerations

If a psychiatrist decides to accept the role of expert witness in a civil case, it is imperative that he or she familiarises him or herself with the provisions of Part 35, Civil Procedure Rules, Practice Direction 35, Guidance for the Instruction of Experts, to give evidence in civil claims and the practice direction on pre-action conduct. An n expert ought to be mindful of the potential consequences for the client of a failure on the expert's part to observe these requirements. The provisions governing experts in criminal cases are contained in Part 33 of the Criminal Procedure Rules and those for Family Proceedings in Part 25 of the Family Procedure Rules and Practice Direction 25A - Experts and Assessors in Family Proceedings.

All expert witnesses need understand that they will be held accountable for their opinions. One way to ensure that this is done appropriately is to pose the following question: Is it possible to prove the theory used and how the expert came to his or her conclusions, when cross-examined? The key to addressing this issue is to be able to answer all the instructor's questions in one's report and/or when giving oral evidence. Although the report may contain influences from other experts, it must ultimately be your opinion and tailored specifically to the individual you are reporting on.

Expert witnesses must avoid relying solely on summaries, abstracts, or excerpts of a nurse, lawyer, or layman anymore than they would do so to make a diagnosis in clinical practice. It is important to stay focused on these basics; this will eradicate the temptation to rely on any assumptions or stereotypes.

Conclusion

There are a lot of factors to consider when agreeing to take on the role of expert witness. The main motive of this chapter is to remind experienced practitioners that, to some extent, it is vital to refer back to basic principles. Although they may seem simple, they have the potential to affect the court proceedings. For example, lack of clarity may lead to additional questioning, which in turn may prolong the proceedings and result in high court costs. Furthermore, this lack of clarity may mislead the court and affect the final outcome of the case. These are just some of the ethical issues that may arise. It is necessary to avoid conflict of interests, adhere to the ethos of confidentiality and sustain the qualities necessary to produce a valid and valuable court report. Consequently, a high level of professionalism and familiarity with all the relevant rules is needed to ensure that expert witnesses reach their full potential.

Acknowledgements

I would like to thank all the authors who have contributed to this book for giving of their time so freely. It is a credit to them all that they can see the value of helping psychiatrists through the increasingly complex landscape which is today's expert witness 'scene'. Especial thanks to Laura Millman who put me in touch with several of the other authors. Thanks, also, go to my wife, Karen, for proof-reading the book.

We Need It By Next Thursday – The Joys of Writing Psychiatric Reports

By Danny Allen

If you have enjoyed this book, and have not already read it, here is a sneak preview of We Need It By Next Thursday:

Introduction

In the quarter of a century or so that I have been a psychiatrist, I have noticed that writing medical reports is a bit of a 'Marmite' subject (for those non-Brits amongst you,

Marmite is a smelly brown substance which some of us like spreading on our toast – you either love it or you hate it). I have seen people who would rather attend long, boring committee meetings than write a short report for the court on one of their patients, and I have seen others who have written highly inadequate reports and not received any payment for them – probably because they recognised at some level that these reports were not worth paying for. I have been writing reports now for over 20 years and, like so many other people, was introduced to them in earnest by doing a forensic psychiatry job. This certainly gave me good training for writing criminal reports, but did not really prepare me for the huge and exciting field of expert witness work which I later discovered existed out there.

Over the years I have been to numerous courses and done huge amounts of training just to ensure that I am appropriately trained and prepared as an expert witness, but there are still surprises and the working environment is still changing, meaning that the work remains as fresh and exciting as it ever was. I don't know why this is; call me an old softy but there is something about this work which calls me back again and again. Although on the surface there are huge similarities between cases, the differences and the human interest just makes me want to come back for more!

From speaking to my trainees over the years, many like the idea of doing medico-legal reports, but have not been given the opportunity to try, whilst others quite clearly, genuinely do not wish to do this. Of course, I have no problem with those who do not wish to do such work, except to point out that from time to time they may be put under quite a considerable amount of pressure to do so, as part of their day-to-day jobs. Therefore it seems like quite a good idea to know how to do it and to be able to avoid some of the pitfalls associated with being an occasional report writer. Indeed the new ways of assessing trainees means that more do get the opportunity and I feel this is an advance. Since training and mentoring junior doctors is something I enjoy as well it has always been a special treat for me when a trainee not only manages to write a good report but gets the appetite for doing so for its own sake.

Many books have been written about medico-legal report writing, some of which I have found extremely useful and I have listed some of these in the bibliography. However, most of these are written from the head and not the heart. I make no bones about the fact that book is based on emotion. It is an account of why I love doing what I do, written in the hope that some of my readers may go on to love doing what they do. In exactly the same way as I love bread and cheese, but prefer cheese sandwiches, so I enjoy clinical work in parallel with my medico-legal work.

One of the joys of doing medicine in the seventies and eighties was the ability to chop and change specialties, almost at whim. I did not enter psychiatry until I had gone through quite a few different medical careers, including orthopaedics, ENT and General Practice, and I have absolutely no regrets about the fact that I did this. What attracted me to psychiatry when I first did it was the huge range of different sub-specialties within it, and so it is with medico-legal work. Looking back now I can see that the reports I did for the criminal courts form only a small proportion of the sorts of work available. In other words, there is probably something for everyone, and for some of us it is the very variety of work which inspires us

In this little book I hope to give you a flavour of what you might expect doing this sort of work, some of the pitfalls and some of the pleasures. Please do not read it expecting some erudite account of the legal and court system – I leave this for my elders and betters. This is a book about the joys of medical report writing. Enjoy!

Chapter 1 – Do I Need the Aggravation?

When I was a senior registrar and started doing medico-legal reports in earnest, I asked one my consultants in general psychiatry who used to do a few reports how he started; he answered straight away, "Buying new shoes for kids is expensive."

Working in the NHS it has become embarrassing for some doctors to talk about money, but if you and I, dear reader, are to be honest with each other, we do rather like being paid well for doing our jobs. And why ever not? Across the world, most doctors charge for their services and there is nothing to be ashamed of in this. There are perfectly ethical ways of doing this and were it not for the motivation to make money businesses, and indeed capitalist societies, would collapse. So if your primary motivation is to make money, do not be ashamed. As I say to my children, "The purpose of education is to allow society to pay you for doing something which you enjoy doing." As professionals, I hope that we enjoy doing our clinical work; I certainly do, and when I worked in the NHS I got paid well for it. In exactly the same way, we should expect to be paid in accordance with our skills if we decide to do medico-legal work.

So that answers your first unspoken question. If we need (or desire) the money we need to do the work to earn it (unless you wish to end up as the subject of a criminal report, of course!). But this does not mean for a minute that this has to be your only motivation because there are lots of other satisfactions to be had in this line of work. For starters, from a public policy point of view, the court system would collapse without experts of one sort or another so we must be performing some sort of useful function even if, from time to time, politicians rail against the expense of paying for our views. Think about this for a moment. Clinical work is important, sure, but how would you feel if, for example, your schizophrenic patient were to be incarcerated for a year for attempting to erect a cross in the middle of the M1. "Can't you see; you would say, this man is obviously unwell and needs treatment". Aha – so you obviously feel impelled to explain to the court the sorts of things which people do when they are deluded and you feel that you could help this man better by admitting him to your ward for 3 weeks. Someone has to explain this to the judge… Why not you? You are, after all, an expert in mental disorder with the ability to communicate and write letters to GPs at least. So how much more difficult can it be to write a court report? And of course, the answer is "Not that much more difficult – but there are a couple of things you need to be aware of…"

And, it is this last bit, quite frankly, which worries (or aggravates) some people. For the occasional report writer, the fear that they might not be aware of some rule or another is enough to put them off the whole thing. But not you my friend! Unless I gave it to you (!) you have probably bought this book because you are flirting with the idea of becoming a medico-legal report writer. To which I say: "Flirt no longer – commit!" Anything worth doing requires some effort and if you wanted a life without aggravation why did you become a doctor? And as a doctor is being a psychiatrist so easy? The key to doing this work is to understand that it is not just an offshoot of clinical psychiatry to be done at a whim but a sort of subspecialty in its own right. Would you become a neuro-psychiatrist without further training? Need I say more?

So; enough talk of aggravation. If you have read this far you probably want to know why it is so much fun; right? Okay, so let's be honest with each other. This is not the same sort of pleasure you get from white-water rafting – okay – it is a little more cerebral than that but then many people would ask you what pleasures you get from conducting a ward round or working within a multi-disciplinary team. What can I tell you? Here is my confession: I get pleasure from the luxury of being able to go through a very full case file, taking notes and forming a hypothesis. The amount of information you get in medico-legal cases is usually much more complete when you see a new patient in out-patients, and you should have (or insist on having) a full copy of the GP notes which can provide lots of rich material.

The next enjoyable part of the process is seeing the client (not a patient – you are not treating them – remember to explain this). However, like a clinical interview, this gives you the opportunity of getting to know a fellow human being, which at the end of the day is what we psychiatrist surely love doing best of all. Although your main job is clearly to write a report I always point out to my trainees that there is often a distinct secondary agenda and this makes for much satisfaction. Nowhere is this more evident than in personal injury cases. The classic case is PTSD; I regularly see people who have soldiered on for two or three years in some considerable distress which they keep thinking will get better – but never does. Make a diagnosis of PTSD, explain that this is an injury and not a mental illness and send them of for treatment by a clinical psychologist and you feel you have done a good day's work. See them 6 months later once treated and you know you are in the right job!

I do a lot of work for the family courts and most of my clients have substance or alcohol abuse problems. Each has a harrowing – but different- story to tell and many of them are hopelessly lacking in insight. However, a small, but significant, proportion has started to 'see the light' and in an even smaller percentage of case, the medico-legal interview can tip them from pre-contemplation to contemplation and sometimes even into real life-changing action. Again I have to tell you that I derive huge pleasure from seeing people for a second time who having listened to what I had to say or who had read and digested my report have taken it upon themselves to do something deep and meaningful to change their lives. These people come back, sit down and talk freely and openly about how they were, what they have discovered about themselves and how they have changed. And very often these are the people who get their kids back in the subsequent court case.

My very last example is of employment cases; these can take a lot of time going through the minutiae of what happened in the workplace and relating this to changes in mental state. But the rewards here too are great. Demonstrating to the client that it was the workplace events which caused their condition can be incredibly validating for them even if you cannot help them do anything about it. But it is also an exercise in very carefully piecing together the evidence which can be very satisfying to those of a slightly obsessional bent.

Whilst I have to confess that my least favourite part of medico-legal work is the actual dictation of the report, the editing of the report in almost every case is a fun pursuit and carefully crafting the conclusions can be very satisfying. I have noticed that some trainees take to this with alacrity whilst others struggle. It is interesting that if you read clinical notes the diagnosis is often vague, or differential, sometimes often crystallising (in often confusing and variable ways) at the point the junior doctor has to put something on the discharge summary. No such vagueness is possible with the medico-legal report and for me this is part of the excitement. The conclusion of any report is your big opportunity to shine. Here you carefully gather in the information you have gleaned, decide whether others may hold a different view, focus in on the questions asked of you (or which you assume the court wants answers to) and then and there, in black and white – pin your colours to the mast. Scary maybe, but what a fantastic discipline!

So; you may say (as someone did to me only the other day) I really want to help my patient or the client I have been sent, but I really don't want to appear in court – that scares me senseless. Oh dear – this is the best bit! How can you tell me that you don't want to dress up in your Sunday best, travel vast distances, taking time off work (which you will need to make up later) and hang around a drafty waiting room for hours on end only to be torn apart by some smart-alec lawyer who has boned up on your subject only minutes before?

Come on – you cannot be serious – this is what I live for! Okay I admit that court is not everyone's cup of tea, but believe me once you have been properly trained and prepared it really can be one of the most rewarding parts of the job and I really do love it! And if you have not been put off – you can read loads more about it later in the book. Even if you never acquire the taste there are some areas of practice where you are much less likely to have to attend – I will probably have to appear in a personal injury case the moment this book is (re)published as some sort of divine retribution but believe me when I tell you I have not been once in twenty tears despite many last minute cancellations.

And if all of the above (never forgetting getting paid) is not enough reason for reading on, how about all those wonderful people you will get to know.

It's a Shrinking Business! – How To Run a Psychiatric Practice

By Danny Allen

This is the third of Danny Allen's books and tells you how to set up a psychiatric practice in the UK. Here is a taster to whet your appetite:

Introduction

Many psychiatrists think that all they have to do, in order to go into private or medico-legal practice, is to show willing and charge money. The truth, unsurprisingly, is much more complex. For a number of years now I have been going up and down the country, giving short talks and whole day workshops on how doctors should run their businesses and I thought it was about time that I put this in writing, to open it up to a bigger audience. It seemed, appropriate, having written a book introducing psychiatrists to the joys of report writing and editing another one by lawyers, that this book should form the third of the trilogy.

This book draws on over twenty years' of experience; most of it found out either along the way or by making mistakes.

Making mistakes is inevitable if you are making sufficient decisions - wise words from Pete Sudbury, my sometime medical director - but some mistakes can be too costly to contemplate and I heard quite a few horror stories from people in workshops, making me think that doctors really should learn a few things before they consider selling their services.

The fact that you have bought (or borrowed) this book suggests a certain degree of insight; others all too frequently carry on blithely, unaware that what they are doing is unlawful. So far I have yet to hear of a doctor being prosecuted for a failure to have employer's liability insurance, but one often hears of doctors pursued by HMRC (Her Majesty's Revenue and Customs) for failure to pay sufficient tax and it is inevitable that, where this crosses the threshold for criminal prosecution, that these doctors will find themselves referred to the GMC (General Medical Council).

In this book I hope you will not only learn about the basics of setting up a business, but also some of the 'tricks of the trade', useful for all doctors, not just psychiatrists. Similarly it is important that you are aware of some of the common pitfalls, particularly in those circumstances where you are in real danger of breaking the law if you do not know what you are doing. In my estimation, private practice and medico-legal work should be pleasurable, lawful and profitable; all three matter, more or less equally.

Another important issue, for UK doctors, is that the vast majority of us work in the NHS and whilst some pay only start a practice on retirement, many more will want to run one in parallel. Indeed, even if you are planning to start after retirement, you will soon gather, on reading this book, that this is not something you should contemplate without a certain amount of planning, so if you are looking for a smooth transition from NHS to private, you may well be advised to start whilst you are still employed. Thus I spend some time talking about how to the rules governing NHS contracts in England, at least, as they pertain to working privately.

So what can you expect from this book? Well, by the time you have finished it you should be in a good position to start your practice on a sound basis. First and foremost, you will have recognised that you are going into business. This may sound totally daft, but my experience suggests that this is not really something which most doctors think about. They think they are doing a bit of doctoring and that the business aspects are for someone else. That someone may be the clinic they are in or the hospital whose consulting rooms they rent – just not them!

Like most other things in medicine it pays to 'read around' your subject. By having a working understanding of the laws and conventions which surround the world of business, you will be in a much better position to think of the things you need to be considering, even if they are new – and new rules are promulgated with monotonous regularity – so that even if everything you read here is not 100% up to date (and how could it be) you will know who to ask to find out the up to date situation. So, by the end of this book, I hope you will be able to:

- Understand why slipping your NHS secretary a tenner for typing a report is unlawful
- Know how to negotiate space for your practice in your job plan
- Realise that an accountant is worth their weight in gold
- Be able to confidently issue tax compliant invoices.
- Have a good understanding of your responsibilities in the business world
- Understand your extra professional responsibilities
- Make sure you train appropriately for your role

- Keep appropriate records
- Make sure you have a mentor or supervisor
- Always be ethical
- Create time to perform your role
- Be open with your employer
- Choose your workplace carefully
- Use modern tools to make yourself more available
- Understand how to employ people legally and ethically
- Use an outsourced payroll function
- Maintain good relationships with your customers
- Make sure you get paid
- Consider how to work with others
- Understand that your business has a value
- Network to get referrals/instructions
- Manage your time and delegate

I hope you enjoy reading this book and benefit from the information in contains. I apologise in advance for any inaccuracies. I have done my best to avoid them but in making the decision to write the book, I have inevitably opened myself up to the possibility that the odd one will slip in!

Chapter 1 - What will I do?

Forgive me for putting this chapter in the book. If you know exactly what you are going to do and how you will do it, you may move straight to chapter 2. However, my experience of talking to people shows that doctors sometimes only have a very vague idea about what they want to do and furthermore how they might go about it. What am I talking about? Well, for example you may be a jobbing adult psychiatrist and think you want to do some private practice. However when you come to set up you realise that you rather like working with people with schizophrenia but that private practice does not enable you to see people with psychosis and, even if they are referred, you lack the necessary team structure to deal with these patients effectively.

Alternatively you might want nothing to do with psychosis in your private practice, considering that you want a complete change from what you do in the NHS. But you may not get referred many patients. So, if you are thinking of seeing private patients you may want to think of going into a niche area.

For doctors who like the idea of medico-legal work, they may think this is something they can just go straight into, but then find themselves embarrassed because they do not know how to compile a report, in particular because they do not know the rules which apply to their chosen field.

Private practice

Many psychiatrists run exclusively medico-legal practices (about which, more below), so deciding to see private patients is tantamount to making a choice – of course there is absolutely no reason why you should not do both but it is as well to think these things through because all choices have implications. First and foremost, as you will find out in chapter 5, is the issue of where you can see patients. You are definitely constrained as to planning permission and, if you do no NHS practice, CQC (Care Quality Commission) rules and therefore, if you do not want to see that many patients, you may well decide that your best option is to get practising privileges at a local private hospital (not necessarily psychiatric) for this purpose.

However, for the purposes of this section, I shall assume that you are very keen on seeing private patients. The first thing to consider is the likely 'market'. There are no real shortcuts. You may need to ask a lot of people, GPs, colleagues etc., and even then you may be none the wiser. At the end of the day you may just need to 'dip your toe in the water'. But this means that you cannot (unless you have lots of money saved) expend vast quantities of money on premises or even staff. Hence renting rooms of one sort or another is probably your best option.

Private practice depends, inevitably on money. The money will come either straight out of the pockets of your patients or from private insurance. In either case, unless you happen to live in a community of lottery winners and landed gentry, this will depend on people being in employment - and a lot less will be in a recession. So being aware of external financial realities is probably as important as knowing who you want to be treating.

So, of course you can be a 'broad-spectrum' psychiatrist, but I suggest that it can be helpful to make known the areas in which you have an interest', even if these are only those areas where you think people will need help – e.g. resistant depression and anxiety. Taking things a stage further how about thinking about what is missing from the NHS. What do people (GPs and patients) ask for but get denied? Obvious answers might include things like adult ADHD (Attention Deficit Hyperactivity Disorder), ASD (Autistic Spectrum Disorder) or mild dementia.

Giving some thought to such matters enables you to plan ahead and, where appropriate, train for your role. I would suggest that, if you want to invest in your future private practice, a two day training course on adult ADHD may be a better use of money, and, as you will discover in the next chapter, totally tax deductible, than renting medical chambers with no certainty of work.

Giving some thought to what you might like to do (and even training for the role) is only the beginning, though, because some roles require you to 'partner' with others and though this may seem simple in theory my experience is that this is the point at which most schemes fall down. I have had numerous meetings with people who have brilliant ideas for 'services' but who do not have either the 'staying power' or the drive to make them come to fruition. These things are not for the faint-hearted, yet the concept of running a 'service' as opposed to just having a practice is very attractive, not only to the practitioners but also to patients and referrers. Well-run services should be able to both inspire confidence and deliver the goods but they take quite a lot of sustained effort to set up.

Medico-legal work

As anyone who has read either 'We Need It By Next Thursday or 'Do You Know a Good Expert?' will know, there is a huge field of medico-legal work out there for psychiatrists but, these days, unlike 'when I were a lad' one would well-advised to prepare and train carefully for the role. Not that I am trying to put anyone off. On the contrary I believe it to be a very fulfilling role and one which I would encourage any young psychiatrist (and maybe even a few old ones) to get into. Just make sure you don't try to run before you can walk.

There are many courses, not least those run by Bond Solon, which exist to teach doctors about medico-legal work. At the point of writing there is no formal 'qualification' for being an expert, but there is a gentle pressure leading in this general direction and, in my book, wherever this is the case, it pays to get ahead of the game, even were it not a good idea in its own right.

At the very least it is as well to be aware that there are rules governing the three main jurisdictions, civil, criminal and family and to go looking for them. These rules require certain wording on reports and, if you fail to include this, you are going to look like a rank amateur. Far better, though, to invest some money in going on a course introducing you to report-writing. If you can find someone who already does this sort of work, why not approach them for some support and mentoring? Most of us are only too keen to help colleagues.

Whatever you decide to do, it makes sense to start at the bottom and work your way up. Whilst you are unlikely to be asked to do a murder case without any experience, solicitors without much experience may just do so and you may feel your ego being stroked. Probably best to resist the temptation on day one!

Cases in the Magistrates' Courts are usually done by local solicitors who may well ask you to report. Sometimes this will be on people who are already your (NHS) patients. If this is the case there are two factors to consider. The first is whether you feel comfortable that there are no conflicts of interest preventing you from reporting – this will apply whether the patient is in the NHS or not. The second, applying only to

NHS patients and to be covered in much greater detail in this book, is to make sure that you deal with any such request in a business-like way, at one remove from the NHS.

In the civil arena the obvious place to start is with personal injury cases involving road traffic accidents. Most of these are handled by agencies, so you can look for agencies active att the time you read this book. I use this phrase advisedly because these businesses have a nasty habit of going out of business without so much as a 'by your leave. It pays to check them out and it pays to make sure you get a formal contractual agreement as to when you will be paid – and if you are not to seriously consider suing them for any money owing before they go bankrupt. More of this below.

As I write, family court work – which used to provide me with a very good living – has all but dried up. Most of us 'in the game' think it will re-emerge, albeit in stilted form but it is a very salutary lesson indeed about the need for flexibility and diversification. The dramatic downturn is partially due to an enforcement of lower fees by the Ministry of Justice, but much more so by an enforced culture change, by that same ministry, which has allowed judges to take a much more assertive role in case management. Whilst we, as experts, may have our views (sometimes pretty trenchant) on our own utility, it matters not a whit if the judges think otherwise.   Anyway this is not the place to rehearse the wide variety of other work available – read one or both of the other books referred to at the beginning of this section if you want to know more!

Other streams of work

What else might psychiatrist do? Well they may teach, they may write (including books!) and they may become SOADs (second opinion approved doctors) appraisers or tribunal doctors. Some of these roles, at least, are clearly paid work but differ from pure employment by the discretion associated with the choice of working hours. Hence they fit well into a 'portfolio career'. Some colleagues feel very strongly that 'time is money' and demand payment for anything. You will have to decide where you sit on the spectrum. I have accepted money for lecturing when it is offered, for example, but I don't insist on it.

By the way, don't expect to make much (if any) money from writing books! Unless you are a great academic (in which case don't expect to be able to retire on the proceeds) you are likely, these days, to spend a small amount self-publishing, then struggle to recoup your costs. But it is really jolly good fun and you should not be put off if you feel the urge. It is great for filling in those gaps where work is slack, patients or clients don't show or that week between Xmas and New Year when everything closes down!

Some psychiatrists, particularly those who have left the NHS, like to combine self-employment with a part-time job. This is often an excellent option. Such jobs are sometimes available within the NHS to people after retirement; you can work up to 2 days - 4PAs (professional activities) without a decrement in your pension. If you are lucky enough to get even one PA this work then you are absolved from having to register with the CQC. Substance misuse jobs in the private sector are often part-time and of course all sorts of other jobs exist. You may be asked to become a (non-executive) director of a charity involved with some area of medical practice. If you are tempted in this direction I would also advise you to train appropriately for the role – the Institute of Directors does some very good courses.

In this chapter we have looked at some of the choices available to psychiatrists who want to go into practice. The main two are private (medical) practice and medico-legal practice, and many will choose to do both together. Having the ability to diversify is important as external constraints may influence what is available at any point in time.

About The Editor

Danny Allen started his medical life doing house jobs in Kettering. After enjoying A & E and orthopaedics he rashly decided to become an 'orthopod'. After working as an anatomy demonstrator at St Marys, he toured the British Isles, failing his primary FRCS exams in some of the most scenic places in the land. After working as a GP in Australia, he decided to train as one and almost immediately did a year of ENT, which he loved and had to tear himself away from. After a spell in medicine and paediatrics in New Zealand, he did his trainee GP year in Basingstoke, but decided to do a spot of psychiatry before becoming a GP principal. Fortuitously, no 6 month jobs were available, so he was invited to join the local psychiatry rotation for a year, and has really never looked back since.

He was a senior registrar on the Bristol rotation before taking up a consultant post in general psychiatry in High Wycombe, where he spent a decade in a community mental health team before working in rehabilitation, assertive outreach, a crisis team and an acute day hospital. In 2005, in the intellectual equivalent of a mid-life crisis, he did a master's in mental health law at Northumbria University, which he thoroughly enjoyed.   Although no academic, he has written over 20 papers on a range of topics. He retired from the NHS in 2011 and worked part time for a year doing substance misuse and psychiatry in an immigration removal centre; an experience which left him with very warm feelings - for the NHS.

From his time as a senior registrar, he has run a business providing medico-legal reports and, over the last decade, has worked with a group of associates to provide a comprehensive service to lawyers.   He is now in private practice with a number of colleagues, but continues to run his medico-legal practice. In 2012 he was elected a Fellow of the Royal College of Psychiatrists, brought out his first book: We Need It By Next Thursday - The Joys of Writing Psychiatric Reports and was elected chair of the Private and Independent Practice Special Interest Group of the Royal College of Psychiatrists. In 2013 he set up 'Professional Healthcare' a service for doctors and other senior staff providing general practice, mental health and occupational health care in one organisation. He is also a Mental Health Tribunal member.

Bibliography

A Handbook for Expert Witnesses in Children Act Cases. The Hon Mr Justice Wall and Iain Hamilton. Family Law 2007

Assessment of Mental Capacity. The BMA and The Law Society. The Law Society 2010

Expert Psychiatric Evidence. Keith Rix. RCPsych Publications 2011

Faulk's Basic Forensic Psychiatry. J. Stone, K. O' Shea, Sarah Roberts, J. O'Grady & A Taylor. Blackwell Science 1999

It's a Shrinking Business - How to Run a Psychiatric Practice. Danny Allen. CreateSpace. 2014

Marketing for the Expert Witness. Catherine Bond and John Leppard. Bond Solon Pubs. 1996

Writing Medico-Legal Reports in Civil Claims – an Essential Guide. Giles Eyre and Lynden Alexander. Professional Solutions Publications 2011

Professionals and the Courts. A Handbook for Expert Witnesses. David Carson. Venture Press 1990

The Expert Witness Marketing Book: How to Promote Your Forensic Practice in a Professional and Cost-Effective Manner. Rosalie Hamilton. Expert Communications 2003

The Little Book on Expert Witness Fees. Chris Pamplin. JS Pubs 2007

The Little Book on Expert Witness Practice in the Civil Arena. Chris Pamplin. JS Pubs 2007

The Little Book on Getting Started as an Expert Witness. Chris Pamplin. JS Pubs 2008

The Expert Witness: A Practical Guide. Catherine Bond, Mark Solon, Penny Harper, Gill Davies. Shaw and Sons 2007

We Need It By Next Thursday – The Joys of Writing Psychiatric Reports. Danny Allen. CreateSpace 2014

Index

www.ingramcontent.com/pod-product-compliance
Lightning Source LLC
Chambersburg PA
CBHW051629170526
45167CB00001B/114

* 9 7 8 1 4 9 7 4 4 9 3 3 6 *